D1743040

Included in the series:*

* Also published in French. Other titles to appear.

Monitoring educational achievement

T.N. Postlethwaite

Paris 2004
UNESCO: International Institute for Educational Planning

The Swedish International Development Co-operation Agency (Sida) provided financial assistance for the publication of this booklet.

Published in 2004 by the United Nations
Educational, Scientific and Cultural Organization
7 place de Fontenoy, F75352, Paris 07 SP

Cover design:
Typesetting: Linéale Production
Printed in France by STEDI

ISBN 92-803-1275-8
UNESCO 2004

Preamble

It is becoming increasingly frequent that ministries of education conduct sample surveys for monitoring educational achievement over time. Usually they conduct such surveys in conjunction with an international study, simply because an international study involves many of the world's leading experts in the field of this kind of research and hence assures the individual ministry of a good technical quality of research for the study. But, occasionally, a ministry decides to 'run' a national study alone.

I have tried to write a short introductory booklet for senior members of ministries of education and others who are not statisticians and not versed in this kind of sample survey research but who need to know about what it is and how they might judge the technical quality of these kinds of studies. It is not a detailed manual on 'how to do studies' of this kind.

In this booklet I have attempted to answer several questions often asked about such studies:

- Why is monitoring of achievement important?
- What are some examples (national and international) of these kinds of studies?
- What are the criticisms of such studies and what are the responses to such criticisms?
- What are the important technical aspects that a study should meet for the results to be trusted?
- What are the implications of such studies for the planning personnel in ministries of education?

The section on the important technical aspects of studies to which attention should be paid has been included because there are some studies appearing that are rife with technical errors to the extent that the results that such studies have reported cannot be trusted. It is for the readers of such studies to decide on the quality of the published research.

In this booklet the international examples have been taken from IEA, PISA and SACMEQ because these studies have been well documented and were easily accessible to the author. There are other international studies. A study of school systems in South America began in 1997 in the Regional UNESCO office in Santiago de Chile. It was the Latin American Laboratory for the Assessment of Quality in Education (LLECE) that actually conducted the work but co-ordinated by the UNESCO Regional Office of Education for Latin America and the Caribbean (OREALC). There are two other programmes: the UNESCO Monitoring Learning Achievement (MLA) that started in 1992, and the educational research programme in the French-speaking African countries known as *Programme d'analyse des systèmes éducatifs de la CONFEMEN* (PASEC). However, it was very difficult to obtain information about various technical points that would have been needed to include these other studies in this booklet.

Of all of the studies it was IEA that was the first and it has been running studies from 1958 until now. The PISA and SACMEQ studies began only in the early 1990s. It should perhaps be pointed out that, in a way, both PISA and SACMEQ grew out of IEA. IEA created a pool of international experts, from which, to a large extent, the teams in charge of PISA and SACMEQ were drawn.

At the international level, Andreas Schleicher, the head of the PISA project, had worked in IEA in Hamburg. It was he, together with John Keeves, who undertook the first calculations of change of achievement over time in the IEA Second Science Study. He was also the Executive Director of the IEA Reading Literacy Study (1989-92). I have been associated with IEA work from 1962 when I became the first executive director of IEA and I was also heavily involved in the IEA Reading Literacy Study.

The sampling statistician responsible for the quality of the probability sampling in the IEA Reading Literacy Study was Kenneth Ross. Kenneth Ross joined the staff of the International Institute for Educational Planning and headed the Monitoring Educational Quality team there. They helped to guide the SACMEQ study until 2004.

At the national level, many PISA National Project Managers were former IEA National Research Co-ordinators (and a number continue to serve in both PISA and IEA studies).

I should like to thank the following people for their suggestions and advice in preparing this booklet: Aletta Grisay (Belgium), François Orivel (IREDU, Dijon, France), Miyako Ikeda (OECD), R. Murray Thomas (USA), Pierre Foy, Dirk Hastedt, and Heiko Sibberns (all from the IEA Data Processing Centre, Hamburg), Cordula Artelt (Max-Planck Institut für Bildungsforschung, Berlin) and Maria Teresa Siniscalco (France).

T. Neville Postlethwaite
Baigts-de-Béarn, France. October, 2004

Fundamentals of educational planning

The booklets in this series are written primarily for two types of clientele: those engaged in educational planning and administration, in developing as well as developed countries; and others, less specialized, such as senior government officials and policy-makers who seek a more general understanding of educational planning and of how it is related to overall national development. They are intended to be of use either for private study or in formal training programmes.

Since this series was launched in 1967 practices and concepts of educational planning have undergone substantial change. Many of the assumptions which underlay earlier attempts to rationalize the process of educational development have been criticized or abandoned. Even if rigid mandatory centralized planning has now clearly proven to be inappropriate, this does not mean that all forms of planning have been dispensed with. On the contrary, the need for collecting data, evaluating the efficiency of existing programmes, undertaking a wide range of studies, exploring the future and fostering broad debate on these bases to guide educational policy and decision-making has become even more acute than before. One cannot make sensible policy choices without assessing the present situation, specifying the goals to be reached, marshalling the means to attain them and monitoring what has been accomplished. Hence planning is also a way to organize learning: by mapping, targeting, acting and correcting.

The scope of educational planning has been broadened. In addition to the formal system of education, it is now applied to all other important educational efforts in non-formal settings. Attention to the growth and expansion of education systems is being complemented and sometimes even replaced by a growing concern for the quality of the entire educational process and for the control of its results. Finally, planners and administrators have become more and more aware of the importance of implementation strategies and of the role of different regulatory mechanisms in this respect: the choice of financing methods, the examination and certification procedures or various other regulation nd incentive structures. The concern of planners is twofold: to reach a better understanding of the validity of education in its own empirically observed specific dimensions and to help in defining appropriate strategies for change.

The purpose of these booklets includes monitoring the evolution and change in educational policies and their effect upon educational planning requirements; highlighting current issues of educational planning and analyzing them in the context of their historical and societal setting; and disseminating methodologies of planning which can be applied in the context of both the developed and the developing countries.

For policy-making and planning, vicarious experience is a potent source of learning: the problems others face, the objectives they seek, the routes they try, the results they arrive at and the unintended results they produce are worth analysis.

In order to help the Institute identify the real up-to-date issues in educational planning and policy-making in different parts of the world, an Editorial Board has been appointed, composed of two general editors and associate editors from different regions, all professionals of high repute in their own field. At the first meeting of this new Editorial Board in January 1990, its members identified key topics to be covered in the coming issues under the following headings:

1. Education and development.
2. Equity considerations.
3. Quality of education.
4. Structure, administration and management of education.
5. Curriculum.
6. Cost and financing of education.
7. Planning techniques and approaches.
8. Information systems, monitoring and evaluation.

Each heading is covered by one or two associate editors.

The series has been carefully planned but no attempt has been made to avoid differences or even contradictions in the views expressed by the authors. The Institute itself does not wish to impose any official doctrine. Thus, while the views are the responsibility of the authors and may not always be shared by UNESCO or the IIEP, they warrant attention in the international forum of ideas. Indeed, one of the purposes of this series is to reflect a diversity of experience and opinions by giving different authors from a wide range of backgrounds and disciplines the opportunity of expressing their views on changing theories and practices in educational planning.

Governments all over the world recognize that education has a central role to play in building nations and in sustaining countries' economic, social and cultural development. Enrolling large numbers of children in schools is, however, not the objective. The objective is to make sure that children learn to a sufficient level to perform well as future citizens in society. A second important concern is to be able to identify which children reach different levels of achievement and what is the profile of those who do achieve at an adequate level, and why. What explains the difference in pupils' achievements? Is it the kind of teachers they had, the type of school they attended, the fact that they had or did not have teaching materials? What is the best predictor of students' educational achievements? Possibly family background, but is teacher training important? Does reducing class size have an impact? Are the enormous expenditures that governments invest in schooling justified? Where should ministries invest in future in order to improve pupils' and students' learning achievements?

In order to answer some of these questions, governments and agencies have become increasingly interested in assessing the learning achievements of pupils and students.

The present booklet, prepared by one of the best specialists in the subject, Neville Postlethwaite, aims at explaining what monitoring learning achievements means; how to recognize a good study from not-such-a-good study. What sort of questions do surveys allow to answer? And which issues do they raise? At a moment when a large number of surveys are conducted at national and international levels, such a booklet is extremely welcome. It should interest all readers wishing to gain or deepen their knowledge and understanding of monitoring learning achievements.

The Institute is very grateful to Neville Postlethwaite, Professor Emeritus of comparative education at the University of Hamburg, for this most interesting monograph, which will allow many non-specialists to understand better what surveys on educational quality are, what information they can provide and what their contribution to policy analysis can be.

Gudmund Hernes
Director, IIEP

Preface

One of the major changes to education systems worldwide during the past two decades is linked to the evaluation of their relative quality through assessment of their outcomes. A 'good' school is no longer defined as a school with excellent levels of school resources, such as a large number of teachers who are well qualified and fairly well paid, small classes, extensive facilities in good conditions, pedagogical material of all sorts, well equipped libraries, access to new information technologies and the Internet, and sports facilities. Rather, a 'good' school is defined by its outputs and not its inputs.

Before this change of perspective occurred, school outputs were not ignored as such, but it was commonly assumed that if school inputs were not limited by budgetary constraints, education outcomes would follow in a kind of automatic way. Schools with the highest levels of inputs would generate better outcomes than schools with lower levels of resources. This assumption has been severely challenged by numerous studies carried out in the 1980s by a certain number of education economists, who clearly demonstrated that in industrialized countries, the variability of school resources was not positively correlated with the variability of educational achievement. In fact, in most developed countries, the correlation between the two categories of variables (input and output variables) was routinely close to zero.

This conclusion entails three major implications: First, as in all economic activities, school inputs have a diminishing rate of return. The classic example is that of textbooks: If there is no textbook in the school, the reading capacity of children remains weak. It increases significantly with the first textbook (per pupil), but the more textbooks are added in the school, the lower the marginal impact. At some point, the usefulness of a new textbook is simply not measurable. The vast majority of schools in developed countries have basically reached the minimum level of resources that allows the learning process to occur and the variability of pupil achievement is due to other factors; some related to the operation of the school and some related to the characteristics of the pupils.

The second lesson is that for a given level of resources, schools do not have the same level of efficiency. This can be because some are better managed than others, but it can also be due to the fact that they do not have the same types of pupils. Some children are more likely to learn properly than others. There are plenty of causes which can explain why certain pupils face learning difficulties: They may be in poor health, they may be less able to learn (innate ability), they may have a mother language different from the working language of the school, they may belong to a family which has less motivation for supporting school values than others, or they may be exposed to a shorter study time, both inside and outside the school. Likewise, high achievers may improve their school competencies by non-school inputs such as private tutoring, active parental support, a linguistic stay abroad or numerous opportunities to partake in out-of-school cultural practices. Most of these factors are strongly socially biased insofar as they require additional private funding, which is hardly accessible to families of low socio-economic status. If schools have an intake composition different enough (a high proportion of high achievers in some schools and a conversely high proportion of at-risk pupils in some others), then the variability of outcomes can be large, whatever the quality of the school management.

The third consequence of assessing school quality by its outcomes is a new approach to designing educational policies. In the past, educational policy-makers used to base their action on their own opinions, values and commitments. More and more, education policies tend to be based on facts, namely the actual effectiveness of schools, and they tend to promote changes that are supposed to improve the learning process for a larger proportion of pupils. The ideal of equal treatment of pupils is progressively being replaced by that of positive discrimination aimed at improving the competences of low achievers.

There is not yet a universal consensus on the nature of school outputs insofar as school objectives as well as school curricula may vary from one school to another or between education systems themselves. However, there are some common denominators, in particular concerning the basics: All education systems are supposed to make pupils able to read, write and count. In addition, they should favour the socialization process of children of a given community, teach them how to behave collectively, and finally help children to become active and responsible adults able to survive properly in their environment.

The significant improvements introduced in the evaluation of educational achievement have mostly addressed the cognitive performances of children in reading, mathematics and sciences. Education systems have many other objectives in areas such as foreign languages, social sciences, art and physical education, civic education, technology, etc. In addition, they have non-cognitive objectives, such as the development of self-esteem, social behaviour, a sense of initiative and creativity. Some opponents to the present efforts for measuring educational achievement claim that most tests that have been used have an excessively narrow focus, tend to ignore a large share of acquired competencies and may result in concentration of actual curricula on areas that are routinely tested. The argument is not without value, but should not lead to the conclusion that new testing approaches should be discarded on these grounds. The only avenue for avoiding this kind of drawback is to extend new testing practices progressively to areas that have not yet been addressed.

A growing number of countries are participating in studies on the monitoring of educational achievement. Yet these countries are more likely to belong to the developed world than to the developing one. One of the purposes of this booklet is precisely to help developing countries enter the process of monitoring educational achievement in a more systematic way in order to guide properly national educational policies and to promote reforms that are more likely to improve the performances of education systems.

Neville Postlethwaite is one of the few leading world specialists in the field. He has played a pioneering role in the development of the appropriate methodologies, tools and analytical procedures for carrying out surveys at the national and international levels. His experience is related to both the developed and the developing world, and no one could have been better placed to write this booklet.

François Orivel
Professor, University of Bourgogne

Contents

Contents

List of abbreviations

ETS	Educational Testing Service
EMIS	Educational management information system
IEA	International Association for the Evaluation of Educational Achievement
IIEP	International Institute for Educational Planning
NAEP	National Assessment of Educational Progress
NFER	National Foundation for Educational Research in England and Wales
NRCs	National research co-ordinators
OECD	Organisation for Economic Co-operation and Development
PIRLS	Progress in International Reading Literacy Study
PISA	Programme for International Student Assessment
SACMEQ	Southern and Eastern Consortium for Monitoring Educational Quality
SAS	Statistical Analysis System
SPSS	Statistical Package for the Social Sciences
TIMSS	Third International Mathematics and Science Study

List of tables

1.   In the case of Vietnam, an examination of the items and how the pupils and teachers performed on them yielded six levels in both reading and mathematics. The number of levels can be different from study to study. In *Tables 2.3* and *3.7* of this booklet an example has been given from SACMEQ, where eight levels were identified.

List of figures

Glossary

Data cleaning: the computer-based process of eliminating errors and inconsistencies in large-scale survey research data files prior to their analysis.

Dummy tables: A dummy or blank table is a table specifying the variables and type of data analysis to be used to complete the table.

Chance score: a score on a multiple-choice test that would be obtained if a student 'guessed' the response to each test question.

Hierarchical linear modelling analysis: a method of analysis that allows researchers to formulate and test explicit statistical models for processes occurring within and between educational units. A two-level model might be pupil and school, or a three-level model might be pupil-class-school or pupil-school-region.

Judgement samples: a non-probability sample that is selected according to the opinion of the researcher concerning what constitutes a 'good' or 'representative' cross-section of the population. No estimates of the standard errors of the values (means or percentages) can be calculated from any sample that is not a probability sample.

Outcome variable: In most cases this is the achievement variable or occasionally an attitude variable.

Probability samples: samples that consist of elements with a known non-zero chance of being selected from a population.

Psychometric properties of items: These include their difficulty indices, their point bi-serial correlations, their differential item functioning, and for groups of items they include such matters as validity and reliability.

Rasch analysis: This refers to the application of the Rasch model (developed by Danish statistician Georg Rasch) as a diagnostic tool in the development and improvement of tests.

Regression coefficients: the coefficients attached to particular variables in order to define a linear combination of variables that is optimally correlated with another variable of interest (the criteria variable).

SAMDEM: the Sample Design Manager Software developed by the IIEP in order to select probability samples of schools.

Sampling error: For a given sample, the sampling error is the error associated with the selection of a particular sample from a hypothetically infinite number of equivalent samples drawn from a target population. In order to measure the sampling error, the standard error for a particular statistic (such as the mean or the percentage) is used. The standard error is calculated by taking the square root of the variance. It can be used to calculate confidence intervals within which the true value for the population is expected to lie.

Sampling weights: Sampling weights are used to adjust for differential probabilities of selection for sample elements. The classic procedure is to assign each element a weight that is proportional to the reciprocal of the probability of including an element in the sample.

SAS (Statistical Analysis System): a software package that is used for the management and analysis of social science data files.

SPSS (Statistical Package for the Social Sciences): a series of programmes for undertaking many different kinds of statistical analyses.

WINDEM: a software system designed to improve the accuracy of transforming data collected using questionnaires and tests into information that can be read by computers.

Zero correlation: no relationship between two variables.

Introduction

The aims of the author of this booklet have been to explain what 'monitoring educational achievement' means, to indicate how achievement has been described in selected national and international studies, to answer commonly raised questions about such studies, to show the kinds of criteria by which studies of this kind are judged and, finally, to list some of the issues that such studies raise for educational planners.

The booklet is concerned with the kinds of special studies that are mounted in order to monitor educational achievement. It is not concerned with ordinary examinations or any form of high-stake testing – this topic was dealt with in a previous issue in this series (Kellaghan and Greaney, 2001). Neither is this booklet a textbook about how to conduct such studies: This would require several volumes.

The examples used in the booklet have been taken from the Vietnam grade 5 survey (Ministry of Education and Training, in press) and from the studies undertaken by the International Association for the Evaluation of Educational Achievement (IEA), the Programme for International Student Assessment (PISA) and the Southern and Eastern Consortium for Monitoring Educational Quality (SACMEQ). This is because these studies were well documented and easily accessible to the author. The author has also used the SACMEQ data archive (Ross, Saito, Dolata and Ikeda, in press) in order to calculate some of the results. Many systems of education undertake their national monitoring exercises by participating in international studies, and this is why there is a focus on international studies in this booklet. As mentioned in the Preface, there are other studies.

Many systems of education, whether national or sub-national, have an educational management information system (EMIS). They collect information at regular intervals, often annually, on how many pupils are in each grade in each school and keep varying amounts of information on each student. They also collect information on the teachers in each grade and on the school heads. They do this for every school in the country and then analyze the data to compare regions, districts and even schools within these subunits. They use these results to plan for further improvement of their systems. Some school systems also conduct school audits of the supplies to schools and in general on the resources available in each school. Again, the data are analyzed to identify shortfalls in schools and also inequity among regions, so that remedial action can be taken to rectify these shortcomings.

Both EMIS and school audits are forms of monitoring in education. Monitoring means observation over time in order to identify changes in the system, whether they are in supplies to schools or in pupil achievement. There is, of course, always a first time, and this is also a part of the monitoring exercise.

A short history

When the President of the United States nominated the first Secretary of State for Education in 1867, it was stated that there should be a yearly report on the state and progress of education (De Landsheere, 1994: 8). Normally, these were reports consisting of several indicators such as pupil enrolments, ages and so on. By the end of the twentieth century, education reports included some 60 to 70 indicators of education. It was primarily in the United States that tests were developed. Several states required all pupils to be tested in several key areas. Agencies supplying such tests were created, the most well known being the Educational Testing Service (ETS) in Princeton, New Jersey. However, it was only in 1969 that *national* sample surveys measuring achievement were undertaken *on a regular basis*.

The first major *national sample* surveys were undertaken in Scotland (Scottish Council for Research in Education) in 1932 and 1947, but they were of intelligence. There was the famous longitudinal study, which started in England in 1948 and which is still continuing, of all children born in the first week of March 1948 (Douglas, 1964), as well as the Swedish study of all children born in Malmö in 1946

(Fägerlind, 1975). In England, there had been some attempt at small-scale surveys to obtain data for analysis for special reports. Pidgeon (1958) had undertaken a small comparative study between England and Queensland in Australia, but these had not been on full probability samples of schools and pupils from the target populations. Thus the international surveys of educational achievement were the first large-scale surveys in which the monitoring of educational achievement was undertaken simultaneously in several countries.

In the mid-1950s, a small group of educators used to meet at the UNESCO Institute for Education in Hamburg, Germany. It was Bill Wall, the Director of the National Foundation for Educational Research in England and Wales (NFER), and formerly of the UNESCO Secretariat in Paris, who was the prime mover of these meetings. These educators, mostly from Europe and the USA, had decided that it was essential to have some information on what pupils in schools actually knew at various points in the school system. Many economists had until then used the proportion of an age group continuing to grade 12 as a proxy measure for educational quality. But this was clearly a very poor measure. The educators meeting in Hamburg decided to try to measure cognitive achievement. They ran a small pilot study in 12 countries and published the results (Foshay, 1962). This developed into the IEA study and there were many IEA studies to follow over the next 40-odd years. This was an international study of achievement, and many countries joined in as it allowed them not only to have a national survey, but also to see how their nations compared with others.

It was also in the early 1960s that the research for the Plowden report (Peaker, 1971) was undertaken and that Coleman was doing the fieldwork for his famous "Equality of educational opportunity" study (Coleman *et al.*, 1966). Sometimes called the "nation's report card", the National Assessment of Educational Progress (NAEP) was created in 1969 to obtain dependable data on the status and trends of achievement in a uniform, scientific manner (Tyler, 1985). But as mentioned above, many countries joined international studies. They did so in order to conduct a national survey of learning achievement and to allow comparisons with similar countries at the same time.

Whether a ministry decides to undertake a national survey or participate in an international survey, the major requirements of the study are the same. However, there are a few more requirements for an international survey, as will become apparent throughout the booklet.

This booklet has been divided into six chapters. First, there is a description of why ministries of education conduct achievement surveys. Second, there are national examples from two developing countries – Vietnam and Kenya – of how they undertook the studies and of some of the results they found to be of interest. Third, there is a chapter on some aspects of international studies such as IEA, PISA and SACMEQ. Fourth, there is a chapter on frequently-asked questions and replies to them. Fifth, there is a chapter describing some of the minimum standards of research for conducting these types of studies. Finally, there is a short concluding chapter on what all of this means for educational planners.

I. Why do countries undertake national assessments or participate in international assessments?

Main reasons

There are several reasons why ministries of education undertake assessments. The two main reasons are:

1. to identify the strengths and weaknesses in the system at a particular point in time; and
2. to track changes in the system over time.

The first time that a ministry undertakes an assessment, it is simply to identify how well the pupils are achieving. When identifying strengths and weaknesses in the system at a particular point in time, ministries are mostly interested in what goes on in the different provinces (or regions or districts) within the country. Examples of the kinds of questions that most interest ministries have been given below. In each case the first set of questions has to do with achievement, but at the same time it is also possible to collect information on other matters in schooling that do not have to do with achievement. Some examples of these kinds of questions have also been given.

a) What proportion of children in each province reach adequate levels of achievement in order to progress to the next grade?
b) What proportion of children reach the levels of achievement thought to be desired in order to be able to cope in society?
c) What are the weak points in achievement?
d) What are the common mistakes that pupils make in test items?
e) Are there gender differences in achievement?
f) Are there differences among different socio-economic groups in achievement?

g) What are the major factors associated with differences in achievement among pupils and among schools?

There are then other kinds of questions that can be asked but which are not directly related to achievement. The questions might be as follows:

a) Is the gender distribution of pupils in each province acceptable?
b) Is the age distribution of pupils in each province acceptable?
c) What kind of, and how much, help is given in the home for pupil learning?
d) What is the distribution of teachers by training and education across provinces?
e) Have all schools in all provinces been visited by inspectors as planned?
f) Do equal proportions of teachers in each province go to the educational resource centres?
g) Do all classrooms in each province have the required number of supplies and equipment?
h) Do all children in each province have the required number of textbooks and materials?

For tracking changes over time, the main interest is in achievement:

a) Has the achievement of pupils improved, remained the same or deteriorated?
b) Has the spread of achievement (among pupils and among schools) decreased?

But at the same time it is important to have measures of changes in other factors to do with learning that might be associated with changes in achievement. The associated questions might well include:

a) Has the composition of pupil enrolment changed? Is the proportion of an age group enrolled in school higher or lower?
b) Have the resources in schools increased?
c) Have the resources in classrooms increased?
d) Has grade repetition decreased?
e) Have home conditions improved?

f)   Is the teaching force better educated and trained?
g)   Are schools inspected more than they were before?

It is up to each ministry to establish the particular questions they wish to have answered by the studies. When the studies are international, it is up to the ministries to ensure that the international studies are able to answer the questions they wish to have answered. In this regard, it is important to stress that individual ministries can always ask extra questions for national purposes (in international studies these are known as 'national options'). A ministry will need to decide whether to conduct a national study alone or whether to participate in an international study. Much will depend on the degree of expertise that exists within a country or whether it can obtain enough outside expertise to undertake the work. It is usually wiser to participate in an international study, as the expertise is readily available. But the price to pay for such a decision is that the nation's results become known internationally. Some ministries do not want this. If a ministry decides towards the end of a project to withdraw its data (or parts of the data), this is not fair to the other countries. To state one example, the scale scores are made on the basis of the item data from all pupils in all countries. If one country then wants to withdraw its data, this means recalculating all of the scales and scores. This is an enormous amount of work and becomes time-consuming and costly. Hence, ministries need to weigh the political cost at the beginning of a study.

First questions that ministries need to ask

Whether the assessment is to be carried out at one point in time only or as a repeat study, it is important for the ministry to decide on:

i)   which grade levels will be assessed;
ii)   which subject matters will be assessed; and
iii) which other variables should be measured at the same time.

Grade levels

Most ministries want to assess the last grade or the penultimate grade of primary school. This is normally grade 5 or 6. Initially, some countries select the last grade of primary for assessment, but when the schools object because of the primary-school leaving examination, then it is the penultimate grade that is selected. Occasionally, a ministry will want to assess lower grades of primary school: either grade 2 or 3. In any assessment exercise it is the data collection that costs a lot of money. There is a difference between a group test and an individual test. Group tests, as the name denotes, are administered to a group of pupils at the same time. In grades 1 and 2, and sometimes in grade 3, the pupils are too young and inexperienced to deal with a group test and a test must be administered individually to pupils. This calls for many more data collectors, all of whom require special training. This becomes very costly. Ministries deciding to test grade levels at the beginning of primary school need to be aware of the problem and the costs involved.

In some cases there is a desire to test at the lower secondary level, and often it is in grades 7, 8 or 9 that testing takes place. At one time a lot of emphasis was placed on the final grade of secondary school. This has not featured recently in international studies because of the many problems involved in comparing systems where many pupils go through to the end of secondary with systems where only small percentages of an age group continue to the end of secondary.

In each case it is up to the ministry to decide which grade or grades to study. To study just one grade costs a lot of money. To study several can become prohibitively expensive.

In international studies it is sometimes said that it is unfair to compare grade groups when the ages in such grade groups differ greatly in the different school systems. The result has often been to compare age groups to see how far each system has brought all of the children born in one year, and then, separately, to use grade groups to identify the relationship of home, classroom and school factors to achievement (more has been written about this in *Chapter V*).

Which subjects?

Most ministries of education seem to be interested in assessing reading, mathematics and science, even at the end of the primary level of education. Although IEA started with several subject matters (reading comprehension, literature, science, French and English as foreign languages and civic education), they seem to have adopted a repeat system of reading, mathematics and science as the core subjects. IEA carries out occasional studies on civic education and technology in education. SACMEQ started with reading and added mathematics. PISA has reading, mathematics and science.

It is unclear whether the major international studies will extend to cover other subject matters or not. It would seem that the national ministries of education are content to have other subject matters assessed only in their national examination centres.

Which other variables should also be measured?

The variables to be measured depend on the kinds of information required by the ministry. Thus, if the ministry is particularly interested in differences in achievement between locals and immigrants, there will be a question on immigrants to determine from which foreign countries they come and how long they have been living in the host country. If the ministry is interested in differences in achievement of pupils in schools having varying amounts of resources (in order to discover if there is a level of resources above which adding further resources will not be associated with any further gain in achievement), then there will have to be a question for which the head will specify which resources in a given list are available and which are not in his/ her school. If the ministry is interested in teacher satisfaction, then a question (or questions) will be needed to measure it, and so on. It is up to each ministry to decide which other variables it wants to be included in such a national or international survey. It is said that it is sometimes difficult to have ministries agree on a set of 'other variables', but in this author's experience all ministries tend to be interested in the level and variance of achievement, and in the relationship of these to other variables. In some cases it will be important to know the relationship of a variable to achievement when one or more other variables have been taken into account. An example of this is the relationship between, say, streaming in schools after the socio-economic status (referred to throughout this booklet as s-e-s) of pupils has been taken into account. Thus, in this case there must also be measures of s-e-s. Even in international surveys there is the national option question, where national ministries can add national questions to international instruments (usually following the international section in the instrument). These extra variables all emanate from the research questions that are listed for a study. The ministries must generate these research questions, and if the study is part of an international study, then they must try to have the research questions incorporated for all countries. If this does not work, then they must use national options. All instruments need to be tried out (piloted) in order to ensure that the instruments and procedures for data collection are in order. Sufficient time must be allowed between the pilot and the main data collection. The ministry and researchers normally agree on this kind of time frame.

In general, the ministry personnel will need to guide those designated to undertake the research on the best source of valid data for the questions in the questionnaires: parents, pupils, teachers, school principals, school inspectors and the like, or some combination of these.

Second questions that ministries need to ask

After having determined who should be tested in which subject areas and which research questions should be posed, the ministries must turn their attention to ensuring that the research within their own country is well conducted. They must ensure that they have people well versed in test and questionnaire construction, not only for constructing national tests and questionnaires but also for co-operating with other constructors in international surveys. If attitudes are to be measured, then of course there must be people available who are well versed in that area.

Second, there must be people available, preferably sampling statisticians, who are experienced in sampling. The whole area of sampling is complex. However, it is also an area where a little knowledge can be dangerous. If there is no such person in the ministry, then they must seek help from outside the country. This is another area where participating in an international survey can be very useful; namely to ensure that good probability samples are drawn and, at the same time, the national researchers can learn from the international experts. All three international surveys – IEA, PISA and SACMEQ – have very good sampling statisticians with a great deal of experience in drawing probability samples in many different school systems. It will be up to the ministry to decide on the level of reporting of the data (district, region or only national) and to specify this to the sampling statistician together with the degree of accuracy required for the selected levels, because this determines the size of sample required to a great extent.

Third, there must be people available who are good in data collection. In general this is the aspect that is usually best conducted. This usually involves:

- the printing of the instruments and checking that no errors have occurred;
- the allocation of unique ID numbers to each pupil, teacher and school principal and ensuring that these are clearly indicated on the instruments (to ensure that the linkage between pupils, teachers and schools can be made);
- the packaging of the instruments for each school;
- the training of the data collectors and the writing of data collection manuals and test administration manuals;
- the organization of the visits to schools, together with the transport to schools and requisite per diems if the data collectors must be at the schools for more than one day;
- the planning of measures to avoid cheating on the tests in the schools;
- the checking of the completed instruments before they leave the schools to ensure that all questions in the questionnaires have been completed; and
- the return and storage of the completed instruments for each school to a central place.

Fourth, there must be a good team for data entry, data cleaning and the calculation of sampling weights.

Finally, there must be people who are trained in data analysis, the interpretation of data and report writing. In some cases ministries do not have people with these skills, or at least not enough people, and again in cases like this it is useful to take part in international studies where national researchers can learn the skills from international experts.

Before leaving this chapter on why countries undertake studies in monitoring educational achievement, it should be mentioned that there are still many countries that do not undertake such studies. In some cases they do not have personnel with sufficient technical knowledge and skills to do the work. In other cases they may be unaware of the benefits of the studies. In some cases involving international studies, they may be afraid of being compared with other countries. These are some of the dangers, but in general many countries do involve themselves in international studies in order to have technically sound research that will provide accurate information that can be used as a basis for improving the system and the efficiency of the investment in education.

II. A quick look at two national studies

Two studies from developing countries have been selected as examples of monitoring educational achievement. The first is a study from Vietnam that was undertaken as a national study only in 2001. The second is a national study from Kenya, but which was undertaken as part of the SACMEQ international study.

The Vietnam study

Towards the end of 1999, the Ministry of Education of Vietnam decided that it should assess educational achievement at the end of primary education. It was interested not only in achievement but in many other issues as well (see *Appendix 1*). But for achievement the major questions were the following:

What was the level of achievement of grade 5 pupils overall and in the various fields of reading and mathematics?

a) *What was the level of grade 5 teachers in reading and mathematics?*
b) *What percentages of pupils reached the different skill levels in reading and mathematics?*
c) *What percentages of pupils reached benchmark levels in reading and mathematics?*
d) *What were the total scores by region and province?*
e) *What were the differences in achievement between: i) pupils in isolated, rural, and urban schools; ii) boys and girls; and iii) different socio-economic groups?*
f) *Were the performances of the pupils' 'elite' (upper 5 per cent) similar in different regions and socio-economic groups? To what extent did the performance 'tails' (bottom 5 per cent) differ across regions and socio-economic groups?*
g) *What were the relationships between teachers' and pupils' performance on the reading and mathematics tests?*

In Vietnam there are five grades in primary education. The Vice-Minister for Education organized a meeting of 36 key people associated with primary education in the Ministry and they developed over 100 research questions that the proposed study should answer. Furthermore, they deemed that the outcome variables should be reading and mathematics. At that time, only 68 per cent of an age cohort survived to fifth grade, but as this was the last grade of primary school, the decision was taken to assess the achievement of this grade rather than a lower grade. At the time there were also some interesting changes taking place: A new curriculum for primary schools was to be introduced. This posed the question of which curriculum should be used to construct the tests. The test construction group based the tests on both curricula, as the idea was to repeat the survey five years later, by which time there would only be the new curriculum in the schools. All key stakeholders viewed the test as fair for all children. The number of hours of instruction varied from a whole day at school to only two or three hours. This was the reality. Nearly all teachers in primary schools were trained at a provincial teacher training college and then became teachers in the schools in the same province. There were 61 provinces; therefore it was decided also to test the pupils' teachers in the same subject matters as their pupils.

The study followed the research questions laid down by the Ministry in every aspect. Work was undertaken in 2000 to construct the test items and questionnaire questions, pilot them in five provinces and finalize them. The main data collection was undertaken on 11-12 April 2001. The sample consisted of 3,660 schools and, with 20 pupils drawn randomly within each school, this made a total of 73,200 pupils in the planned sample. The Ministry wanted to have good estimates of achievement for each province as well as for the eight regions in the country. Hence 60 schools, with a probability of selection proportional to the enrolment in grade 5, were drawn from within each province. Sampling weights were to be used for the differences in enrolment among provinces at the analysis stage. However, the data collection was a massive undertaking involving over 4,000 persons. There was one data collector per school, and then about 400 more who were standing by as reserves or acted as supervisors to check the quality of the data collection. Two teams of data entry people were trained. A further team of data cleaners was trained and, finally, a team for the analysis of the data was available. Twenty computers (PCs) were available for the work. The Vietnam team was able to have help for the sampling, calculation of sampling weights and standard errors of sampling as well as for data cleaning from the Monitoring Education Quality team at the International Institute for Educational Planning (IIEP) in Paris.

Some of the results

Test results can be used in various ways to describe performance. In the Vietnam study, three different approaches were used. The first consisted of establishing levels of skill competency, the second of functional levels – for being able to cope in the next grade or in society – and the third was using a mean and standard deviation to describe pupils' achievement. Examples have been presented for all three.

An example of skill levels

The first approach consisted of examining the difficulty levels of items and then seeing how these items clustered together to form a hierarchy of skills. By describing the skills needed in each cluster it was possible to establish six levels of skills in each subject matter, and *Table 2.1* shows the percentages of pupils reaching the different levels together with the accompanying standard error of sampling. What is important about this approach to achievement data is that it is possible to see which kinds of pupils and how many of them can or, as the levels are hierarchical, cannot perform different skills in reading. It can be seen that there were more pupils at very low levels of reading than pupils at very low levels of mathematics. Indeed, levels 1 and 2 can be regarded as pre-reading, and in this sense the 19 per cent of children at these levels in grade 5 was worrisome. The percentages of pupils and accompanying sampling errors have been presented for each *province* and *region* in *Appendix 2*.

It can be seen that the distribution of pupils at the lower skill level was not even: In some provinces there were many pupils at a low skill level while in other provinces there were few. Clearly this information can be used to design targeted intervention programmes aimed at redressing highly specific skill deficits of groups of pupils.

There were, for instance, more than 10 per cent of pupils at level 1 (the lowest level) in reading skills in Cao Bang, Tuyen Quang, Hoa Binh, Kon Tum, Tra Vinh and Bac Lieu. Such prevalent low skill levels in reading at the end of primary school clearly require intervention before these pupils enter the community as independent citizens or begin their lower secondary education and expect to be independent learners. These incidences of low skill levels were prevalent in four regions: the North-West, the North-East, the Central Highlands and the Mekong Delta region. On the other hand, there were provinces where more than 20 per cent of the pupils assessed were at the highest level of reading and more than 35 per cent at the highest levels of mathematics. These were found in Ha Noi, Hai Duong, Hung Yen, Thai Binh, Bac Ninh, Quang Ninh, Da Nang and Ho Chi Minh. All of them were in the highly industrialized urban regions of Vietnam.

Table 2.1   Percentages of pupils reaching different skill levels in reading and mathematics in grade 5 in Vietnam, 2001[2]

	Reading skill levels	Percentage	SE
Level 1	Matches a text at word or sentence level aided by pictures. Restricted to a limited range of vocabulary linked to pictures.	4.6	0.17
Level 2	Locates a text expressed in short repetitive sentences and can deal with text unaided by pictures. Type of text is limited to short sentences and phrases with repetitive patterns.	14.4	0.28
Level 3	Reads and understands longer passages. Can search backwards or forwards through a text to find information. Understands paraphrasing. Expanding vocabulary enables understanding of sentences with some complex structure.	23.1	0.34

2.   In the case of Vietnam an examination of the items and how the pupils and teachers performed on them yielded six levels in both reading and mathematics. The number of levels differ from study to study. In *Tables 2.3* and *3.7* of this booklet an example has been given from SACMEQ, where eight levels were identified.

Table 2.1   (continued)

	Reading skill levels	Percentage	SE
Level 4	Links information from different parts of a text. Selects and connects text to derive and infer different possible meanings.	20.2	0.27
Level 5	Links inferences and identifies an author's intention from information stated in different ways, in different text types and in documents where the message is not explicit.	24.5	0.39
Level 6	Combines a text with outside knowledge to infer various meanings, including hidden meanings. Identifies an author's purposes, attitudes, values, beliefs, motives, unstated assumptions and arguments.	13.1	0.41
	Mathematics skill levels	Percentage	SE
Level 1	Reads, writes and compares natural numbers, fractions and decimals. Uses single operations of adding, subtracting, multiplying and dividing on simple whole numbers. Works with simple measures such as time. Recognizes simple 3D shapes.	0.2	0.02
Level 2	Converts fractions with denominator of 10 to decimals. Calculates with whole numbers using one operation (adding, subtracting, multiplying and dividing) in a one-step word problem. Recognizes 2D and 3D shapes.	3.5	0.13
Level 3	Identifies place value. Determines the value of a simple number sentence. Understands equivalent fractions; adds and subtracts simple fractions. Carries out multiple operations in correct order. Converts and estimates common and familiar measurement units in solving problems.	11.5	0.27
Level 4	Reads, writes and compares larger numbers; solves problems involving calendars and currency, area and volume. Uses charts and tables for estimation. Solves inequalities. Transformations with 3D figures. Knowledge of angles in regular figures. Understands simple transformations with 2D and 3D shapes.	28.2	0.37

Table 2.1 (continued)

	Mathematics skill levels	Percentage	SE
Level 5	Calculates with multiple and varied operations. Recognizes rules and patterns in number sequences. Calculates the perimeter and area of irregular shapes. Measures irregular objects. Recognizes transformed figures after reflection. Solves problems with multiple operations involving measurement units, percentage and averages.	29.7	0.41
Level 6	Solves problems using periods of time, length, area and volume. Uses embedded and dependent number patterns. Develops formulae. Recognizes 3D figures after rotation and reflection. Recognizes embedded figures and right angles in irregular shapes. Interprets data from graphs and tables.	27.0	0.6

Source: Ministry of Education and Training, in press: Table 2.1.

An example of levels of functionality

As well as having information on who can and cannot do what in reading, some countries wish to have information on some notion of how well the pupils can function in school and society. Hence, in Vietnam a second way of looking at the item data was to ask the Ministry's reading and mathematics subject-matter groups to classify the items in the test into those considered pre-functional for being able to operate in Vietnamese society, those regarded as functional, and those representing a level where the pupils would be able to learn independently in grade 6 (see *Table 2.2*).

Table 2.2   Percentages and sampling errors of pupils at different functional levels of reading and mathematics in grade 5 in Vietnam, 2001

Functionality		Reading		Mathematics	
		%	SE	%	SE
Independent	Reached the level of reading and mathematics to enable independent learning in grade 6.	51.3	0.58	79.9	0.41
Functional	Reached the level for functional participation in Vietnamese society.	38.0	0.45	17.3	0.36
Pre-functional	Not reached the level considered to be a minimum for functional purposes in Vietnamese society.	10.7	0.3	2.8	0.13

Source: Ministry of Education and Training, in press: Table 2.6.

Results of this kind were also produced for each province. The results could also be classified by urban/rural populations, by different socio-economic groups and so on. An example of these functional levels for pupils in isolated areas, rural areas and urban areas for reading and mathematics has been presented in *Figure 2.1.*

Figure 2.1 Relationship between school location and functionality level of achievement in Vietnam, 2001

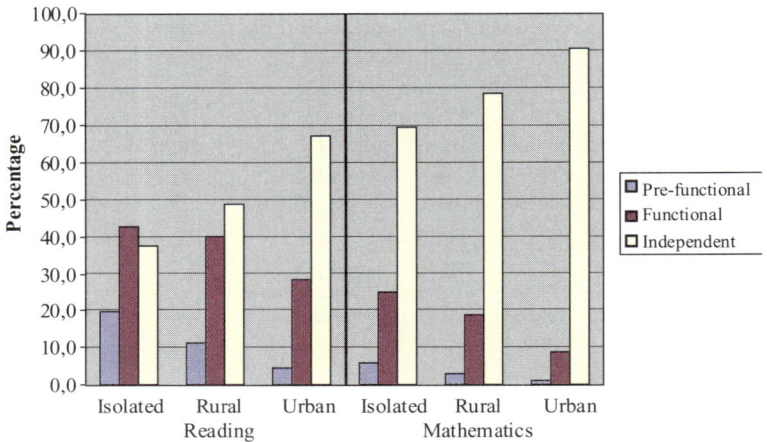

Subject and school location

Source: Ministry of Education and Training, in press: Figure 2.4.

An example of scores based on all items

A third way of dealing with item data is to create a score based on all the items in the test. A mean and standard deviation can be calculated for the scores, and in most cases the mean is designated to be 500 and the standard deviation to be 100. This is what was done in the case of Vietnam. These scores can be useful for comparisons among groups and also for correlational purposes. An example of the boys' and girls' scores in different regions and in Vietnam as a whole has been presented in *Figure 2.2*. The score is on the vertical axis and the provinces have been given on the horizontal axis. It can be seen that girls outperformed boys in Vietnam as a whole, as well as in each region.

These same kinds of scores can be used to examine the relationship between teachers' and pupils' scores. It was pointed out that it was thought that there may have been a problem with teachers being trained in their own province and then teaching in the schools in that province. It was a problem because there was no mechanism for ensuring that the same standards of subject-matter learning had been achieved throughout the country.

Figure 2.2 Boys' and girls' mean reading scores by region in Vietnam, 2001

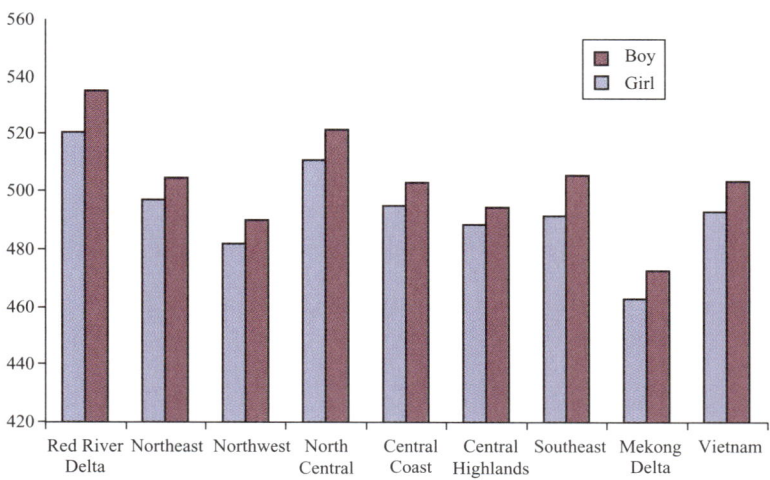

Source: Ministry of Education and Training, in press: Figure 2.10.

Figure 2.3 Relationship between provincial teachers' and pupils' mean reading scores in Vietnam, 2001

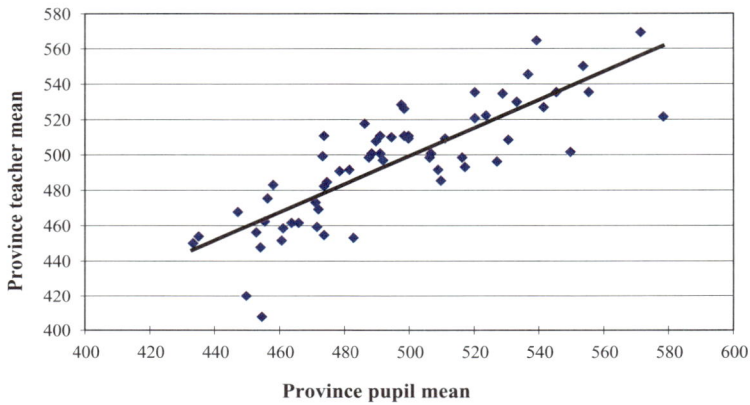

Source: Ministry of Education and Training, in press: Figure 2.13.

Figure 2.4 Relationship between provincial teachers' and pupils' mean mathematics scores in Vietnam, 2001

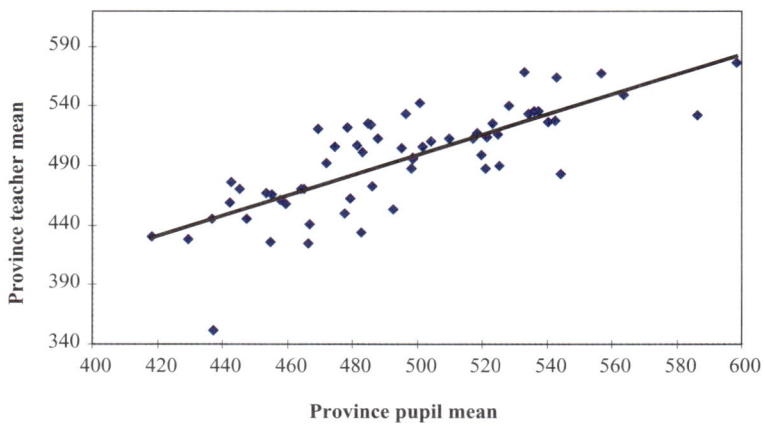

Source: Ministry of Education and Training, in press: Figure 2.14.

The relationships between provincial teachers' mean performance and provincial pupils' mean performances have also been shown in *Figures 2.3* and *2.4*. The province where both pupils' achievement and teachers' knowledge were very low is Lang Son, where province teachers were weak in both mathematics and reading skills, and this was also associated with low pupil performances. The correlations at the province level between pupils' and teachers' scores were 0.82 for reading and 0.78 for mathematics. Pupils taught by teachers with low skills in mathematics and reading had a serious handicap that needs to be overcome. The most likely reason why there were large differences among provinces in teacher subject-matter knowledge was that teacher training was conducted in a teacher training college within a province. There was no national certification examination for teachers in the different subject matters (as there had been before) and hence different provinces developed different standards. This was shown to be related to the differences in pupils' achievement among provinces, and the national authorities should perhaps consider remedying this problem. It was also clear that the standards of the reading and mathematics knowledge of teachers, in the low scoring provinces in particular, had to be improved.

These were but some examples of some of the achievement data presented in the Vietnam report (Ministry of Education and Training, in press). They are sufficient to give an idea of what was done, and it is obvious how such data could be of use to the national authorities as well as to some provincial authorities.

Many other analyses were undertaken in the report concerning the inputs and processes in the schools. The between-school variation, not only in achievement but also in material and human resources, was also reported and finally a hierarchical linear model was conceived and calculated in order to show the effects of many different variables on achievement.

This was the first survey ever undertaken by the Ministry of Education in Vietnam. It was paid for by a World Bank loan. The local teams – mostly from the National Institute for Educational Sciences (NIES), now defunct – were helped by a small team of foreigners in the construction and sampling of the test and in the data entry, cleaning and analysis processes. Unfortunately, the teams that had reached a good level of proficiency were disbanded after the exercise for unknown reasons. It takes a lot of time and training to have good research teams. Once they have been disbanded it is very difficult to re-form them or build them up again. Every effort should be made to keep them.

The Kenya study

Fourteen countries, including Kenya, participated in the SACMEQ II study (see *Appendix 3*). More information on SACMEQ has been presented in *Chapter III* of this booklet. The instruments were developed collectively and the participating countries were helped in the sampling, the data recording and cleaning and the analyses phases of the work by the Monitoring Educational Quality team at the IIEP.

Each country communicated the research questions that it wanted answered and a consensus was quickly reached on the research questions for the whole study. These have been reproduced in *Appendix 4*. On the basis of the research questions a series of dummy tables (blank tables) was developed in order to guide the whole study. At an early meeting of all national research co-ordinators (NRCs), two parallel working groups were formed that focussed on test and questionnaire construction. The test construction group completed a comprehensive analysis of the official curricula, school syllabi, textbooks and examinations that were used in SACMEQ countries. This analysis was used to construct test blueprints as frameworks for writing a large pool of test items for pupils and teachers in both reading and mathematics. The questionnaire group concentrated on using the dummy tables to guide the construction of questionnaires for pupils, teachers and school heads.

By the end of the meeting, the following data collection instruments had been drafted: pupil reading and mathematics tests, the pupil questionnaire, teacher reading and mathematics tests, the teacher questionnaire and the school head questionnaire. In addition, draft manuals had been prepared for the NRCs and data collectors. The test items were trialled in all countries on judgement samples of schools and grade 5 pupils, both classical and Rasch item analyses were carried out and final tests produced.

The desired target population definition for the SACMEQ II Project was "All pupils at grade 6 level in 2000 (in the first week of the eighth month of the school year) who were attending registered mainstream primary schools." Each NRC produced a sample frame and the Monitoring Educational Quality team in Paris taught all NRCs how to draw a sample using a programme called SAMDEM. Kenya took part in the above exercise, but excluded schools with fewer than 15 grade 6 pupils and special schools, which amounted to 3.7 per cent of all pupils. There were 185 schools and 3,700 pupils in the planned sample, and in the achieved sample there were 185 schools and 3,299 pupils (an overall response rate of 89 per cent). The reason for the pupil shortfall was that, in some remote areas, some of the children drawn in the within-school sample were not attending school. In 1998, Kenya had also administered the SACMEQ I instruments, and this allowed comparisons of achievement over time. The intra-class correlation (the amount of between-school differences in reading and mathematics as a proportion of the total between-pupil variance) in Kenya was relatively high (0.45 for reading and 0.38 for mathematics). This meant that a sufficient number of schools had to be included in the sample to cover all of the between-school variation. The data collection was undertaken by about 200 data collectors, the data entered and cleaned and analyses undertaken. In the next chapter, reference has been made to changes in scores over time. In this chapter, some of the highlights of the results of the 2000 study have been presented.

An example of skill levels

First, an example of the percentages of pupils reaching different skill levels by province has been given in *Table 2.3*. In this case there were eight levels for the pupils and the teachers. In general the teachers were at levels 7 and 8, but it can be seen that some of the pupils also reached these levels. As in Vietnam, the Kenyan authorities also wanted to know the percentage of pupils at the different levels.

Table 2.3 Percentages and sampling errors of pupils reaching competence levels by province in grade 6 in Kenya, 2000

Percentages of pupils reaching literacy competence levels

Province	1 %	1 SE	2 %	2 SE	3 %	3 SE	4 %	4 SE	5 %	5 SE	6 %	6 SE	7 %	7 SE	8 %	8 SE
Central	0.2	0.16	3.5	1.14	5.9	1.20	19.6	3.12	30.8	2.84	21.0	2.78	14.4	3.15	4.6	2.37
Coast	1.3	0.94	4.9	2.25	8.7	2.80	18.2	4.91	19.5	2.88	21.7	3.95	20.3	4.28	5.4	1.74
Eastern	0.4	0.31	3.2	1.36	6.6	2.11	16.9	3.37	21.9	2.43	23.9	3.08	20.9	3.75	6.2	1.88
Nairobi	0.8	0.58	1.3	0.71	4.2	1.97	4.6	1.13	16.5	2.69	21.6	2.85	32.3	3.91	18.6	4.02
N/Eastern	1.3	0.77	11.2	2.88	15.7	2.61	20.7	3.09	19.3	2.20	15.4	2.28	11.6	3.05	4.7	1.99
Nyanza	1.1	0.67	3.6	1.13	12.8	2.81	25.2	3.09	28.7	3.09	14.9	2.75	9.8	2.53	4.0	1.47
R/Valley	2.2	0.92	7.4	2.01	17.2	2.99	18.8	2.50	20.8	2.33	18.6	2.77	10.2	2.24	4.8	2.00
Western	0.8	0.42	4.2	1.53	10.8	1.96	27.5	2.71	30.9	2.60	16.0	2.54	6.8	1.82	2.9	1.65
Kenya	1.0	0.27	4.6	0.66	10.8	1.02	20.4	1.24	25.3	1.09	19.2	1.18	13.6	1.18	5.1	0.81

Source: Ross, in press.

It can be seen that although only 5.6 per cent of pupils in Kenya as a whole were at level 2 and below, this figure was considerably higher in the North-Eastern province (12.5 per cent). At level 3, it was the North-Eastern, Nyanza and Rift Valley regions that were higher than other provinces. On the other hand, more pupils in Nairobi attained the higher competence levels than pupils in other provinces. It is this kind of information that is important for planners so that they know where to put more effort.

An example of minimum and desirable levels of mastery

A second approach was taken with scores. In SACMEQ I, two levels of mastery had been defined by specialist reading panels. It was the average of these SACMEQ I levels (including Kenya) that were used for the calculations for SACMEQ I and SACMEQ II results. The items selected to represent the minimum level were to indicate the ability to survive in Kenyan society, whereas for the desirable level the items were to represent the capacity to continue to grade 7 and cope well at that level. The percentages of pupils reaching the minimum and desirable levels of mastery in reading have been given in *Table 2.4* for SACMEQ I and II.

It can be seen that there was an apparent decline in the percentage of pupils reaching the minimum level of mastery from 69.7 per cent in 1998 to 65.5 per cent in 2000. However, the difference of 4.2 per cent was not statistically significant at the 95 per cent level. The increase at the desirable level was also not statistically significant. The implication of these results is that in the year 2000, 34.5 per cent of the pupils enrolled in grade 6 did not meet the minimum level of mastery, while 79.1 per cent did not reach the desirable level of mastery. Nevertheless, in six out of the eight provinces there was an increase in the percentage of pupils reaching the desirable level. It may be that the SACMEQ I specialists set the desirable level too high, but the minimum level was very basic. The Kenyan reading specialists will need to review the items used to define the two levels and the poor results. It will also be important for the specialists to develop strategies so that larger percentages of grade 6 pupils reach the minimum level. Ultimately, the figure should reach 100 per cent.

Table 2.4 Percentages and sampling errors of pupils reaching minimum and desirable levels of mastery in reading (SACMEQ I and SACMEQ II) by province in Kenya

| Region | SACMEQ I (1998) | | | | SACMEQ II (2000) | | | |
| | Pupils reaching minimum level of mastery | | Pupils reaching desirable level of mastery | | Pupils reaching minimum level of mastery | | Pupils reaching desirable level of mastery | |
	%	SE	%	SE	%	SE	%	SE
Central	84.1	3.00	18.6	2.93	74.3	4.14	20.6	5.18
Coast	72.8	5.42	21.5	5.14	69.4	7.70	27.3	6.33
Eastern	70.1	6.17	18.5	5.20	74.0	5.61	30.9	5.67
Nairobi	88.7	2.48	53.8	6.62	88.7	2.44	54.5	6.01
North-Eastern	49.8	8.91	12.8	4.13	54.1	5.13	18.6	4.07
Nyanza	50.1	6.41	7.0	1.95	60.2	5.55	15.1	4.02
Rift Valley	76.6	4.90	25.2	5.85	56.8	5.87	17.3	4.08
Western	61.8	6.51	13.6	3.08	58.6	4.56	10.8	3.46
Kenya	69.7	2.29	18.5	1.86	65.5	2.25	20.8	1.92

Source: Ross, in press.

Another way of using achievement data is to examine the differences between subgroups of pupils. *Table 2.5* presents the percentages and sampling errors of subgroups of pupils reaching these levels.

Table 2.5 **Percentages and sampling errors of pupils reaching minimum and desirable levels of mastery in reading by subgroups of pupils (SACMEQ I and SACMEQ II) in grade 6 in Kenya**

Sub-groups	SACMEQ I (1998)				SACMEQ II (2000)			
	Pupils reaching minimum level of mastery		Pupils reaching desirable level of mastery		Pupils reaching minimum level of mastery		Pupils reaching desirable level of mastery	
	%	SE	%	SE	%	SE	%	SE
Gender								
Boys	69.2	2.65	19.8	2.35	64.3	2.46	21.9	2.22
Girls	70.2	2.47	17.1	1.94	66.7	2.48	19.6	2.09
Socio-economic level								
Low s-e-s	66.1	2.79	14.6	1.80	57.9	2.57	12.7	1.56
High s-e-s	74.9	2.58	24.1	2.90	76.6	2.30	32.5	3.02
School location								
Isolated/rural	64.6	2.99	12.8	1.73	60.2	2.76	13.8	1.99
Small town	75.9	4.84	21.5	4.41	71.6	5.96	26.6	4.17
Large city	88.5	2.10	48.6	6.59	82.9	3.46	47.8	6.13
Kenya	69.7	2.29	18.5	1.86	65.4	2.26	20.9	1.93

Source: Ross, in press.

It can be seen that there was no significant difference between the percentages of boys and girls reaching the mastery levels at each period of time. Furthermore, the percentage of boys reaching the minimum mastery level in SACMEQ II was not significantly different from that of SACMEQ I.[3] The differences between the percentages of pupils in different socio-economic groups attaining the different mastery levels were significant. When comparing the differences between the pupils living in isolated areas/villages and those in small towns and in urban areas, the percentages tended to rise the more urban the setting.

An example of multivariate analysis

However, there were variations among provinces and among schools within provinces – not only as regards teacher subject-matter knowledge, but also as regards other variables. If the planners are to be guided by the research as to where to place more effort in their attempted improvements to the school system, it is useful to conduct some multivariate analyses in order to disentangle those variables that are more related to achievement from those having weaker relationships with achievement. In many countries, parents tend to send their children to schools that are attended by children of the same social class as their own. Well-to-do schools usually have more school and classroom resources, and often more experienced teachers. The poorer children are in schools with fewer resources and less qualified teachers. If the researcher wishes to see if there is a relationship between

3.   There are several methods of calculating the significance of the difference of two means. One quick way has been presented here for the difference of the two percentages (SACMEQ I and SACMEQ II, two independent samples) for boys, which, in this example, is 4.9 (69.2 - 64.3). Then square the sampling error of the first mean and add it to the square of the sampling error of the second mean. This yields 13.075. Take the square root, which yields 3.61. This is one sampling error of the difference of the two means. To be confident 95 per cent of the time that the difference is really different, multiply the 3.61 by 2. This yields 7.22. This is larger than the difference of the two means and hence the difference is not significant at the 95 per cent level. If the samples are not independent (say boys versus girls in SACMEQ II because they are often in the same schools), then a special form of so-called 'jackknifing' is required for good estimates of the standard error of the difference.

resources and achievement, it is usually desirable to do this after the effect of home background has been removed. Hence, it is important to undertake some form of multivariate analysis. The Kenyan team undertook a hierarchical linear modelling analysis of the data and found that there were several variables that were more strongly related to pupil achievement than others (see *Table 2.6*).

Table 2.6 Important variables predicting reading and mathematics achievement in grade 6 in Kenya (SACMEQ II)

Variables	Reading	Mathematics
Among provinces		Teacher mathematics score
Among schools	PTR (negative)	PTR (negative)
	Home background	Home background
	Pupil behaviour	Pupil behaviour
		Teacher training
Among pupils	Age	Age
	Home background	Home background
	Lack of materials	Lack of materials
	Grade repetition	Sex

PTR = pupil-teacher ratio.
Source: Ross, in press.

It can be seen that teachers varied in their mathematics scores among provinces and that this was related to provincial differences in pupils' achievement. The variables associated with differences among schools were more or less the same for both subject matters. Schools with smaller pupil-teacher ratios[4] had higher scores than schools with larger pupil-teacher ratios. Schools with pupils from more advantaged home backgrounds performed better than schools with pupils from poorer home backgrounds. Schools with fewer behavioural problems

4. Pupil-teacher ratio is not to be confused with class size. The pupil-teacher ratio is the total enrolment of the school divided by the number of teachers (full-time equivalent) in the school. In a sense, it is a measure of how well-off the school is in terms of teachers. Class size is the number of pupils in a class or the average number of pupils in a class in a school. A school may have seven teachers and only six classes.

(as perceived by the head teacher) performed better than schools with more behavioural problems. Since these variables were associated with differences in schools' scores in both subject-matter areas, they are important. As schools with pupils from more advantaged home backgrounds also tend to perform better (correlation of 0.566 at the school level), social segregation among schools is a problem that the authorities will have to deal with. Schools with teachers who had more professional training were estimated to perform better in mathematics (but not in reading) than schools with untrained teachers or teachers who had little professional training.

The differences among pupils within schools were associated with age (younger pupils performed better), home background again, and a lack of materials (pencils, pens, exercise books, notebooks, erasers and rulers). Pupils with fewer resources scored less well than pupils with more materials. The data for this study were collected in 2000, and since then the Kenyan Ministry of Education has ensured that all pupils have enough materials. In reading, those pupils who had repeated a grade performed less well than those who had not repeated a grade. In mathematics, girls performed less well than boys.

These are the facts emerging from the analysis that the Ministry needed to know. The Kenyan researchers provided some suggestions to the Ministry as to what to do, but any action taken by the Ministry to improve the school system at the end of primary schooling will depend on funding. It will need to devise policies that are acceptable to the teacher unions and the electorate, and do so in such a way as to avoid any major upheavals in the schools.

III. Some international studies

Three large international organizations have conducted international achievement studies in education that are very well known.[5] These are SACMEQ, PISA and IEA.

SACMEQ

SACMEQ was created as a capacity-building (training) programme in the skills of assessment research. It used a co-ordinated set of national studies for the trainees to have 'hands-on' training. The aims of the research conducted were to monitor changes in achievement as well as to identify weaknesses in the systems in terms of inputs to and processes in education, making policy suggestions about what the various units in ministries of education might do to improve the system. SACMEQ differs from other studies in that it takes a great deal of trouble to discover the major policy concerns that its ministries have and the research questions they wish to have answered. It is these research questions from the ministries that form the basis of the SACMEQ studies. Not only does the ministry have a lot to say about what questions the research should answer, but in the final formulation of the policy it provides suggestions for improving the system. SACMEQ selected grade 6 as the target population. The reason is that it is the last grade of primary education in some countries and in others the penultimate grade of primary education. It is clear that in many African countries there is a great deal of grade repetition; children are in and out of school depending on home demands and the ability of parents to pay school fees. Thus there is a huge age variation in grade 6. For the most part, however, grade 6 means the sixth year of schooling, even though it may have taken some children more than six years to reach

---

5.   As mentioned in the *Preface*, there are also other studies. However, it is the studies from IEA, PISA and SACMEQ that are best known to this author and hence used here as examples.

that point. The major focus are pupils' (and teachers') achievements in literacy and numeracy. The first wave of testing (SACMEQ I) took place in 1995, with seven countries participating. In the 2000 testing (SACMEQ II), 14 countries took part. Zimbabwe was the fifteenth member of SACMEQ but did not participate in the 2000 testing. One interesting feature of the governance of SACMEQ is that the Assembly of Ministers, the overall governing committee of SACMEQ, consists of the ministers of education of the participating countries.

An example of change in achievement over time

Two examples of changes in achievement in terms of minimum and desirable levels of achievement were given for Kenya in *Tables 2.4* and *2.5*. Another example concerns changes in scores between SACMEQ I and SACMEQ II for those countries common to both studies. The mean of all countries was 500 and the standard deviation was 100. SACMEQ I took place in 1995/1996, however Malawi and Kenya were tested in 1998. SACMEQ II took place in 2000 with the exceptions of Mauritius and Malawi, where testing occurred in 2001 and 2002 respectively. Many of the test items were the same, and the two sets of tests were equated and a single scale produced. Only six countries that had participated in SACMEQ I also participated in SACMEQ II. These results have been presented in more detail in this article as the author had access to the data files (Ross *et al.*, in press). Overall results by country have been presented in *Figure 3.1*.

**Figure 3.1 Changes in literacy scores between
SACMEQ I and II**

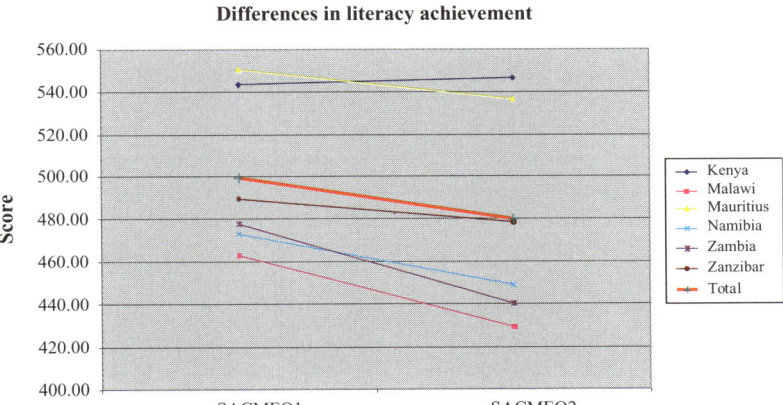

Differences in literacy achievement

Source: Ross *et al.*, in press.

It can be seen that Kenya and Mauritius were at about the same level of achievement and that, with the exception of Kenya, all the countries' scores declined over the five-year period. The thick red line represents the overall score for all of the six countries. However, when the standard errors of sampling are taken into account, it was only in Malawi, Namibia, Zambia and Zanzibar that the differences were significant. It should be remembered that there were only two years between SACMEQ I and II in the case of Kenya, whereas for Mauritius there were six years (1995-2001). It should also be pointed out that the net enrolment ratios for the six countries in 2000 were: Kenya = 68; Malawi = 81; Mauritius = 93; Namibia = 68; Zambia = 66; and Zanzibar = 50 (UNESCO Institute for Statistics, 2004). It is also possible to present the data in a different way (see *Figure 3.2*).

Figure 3.2 Changes in reading scores between SACMEQ I and SACMEQ II

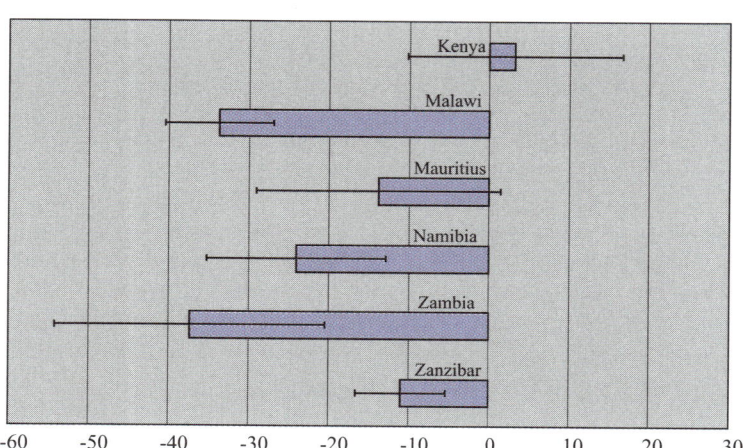

Source: Ross *et al.*, in press.

This figure is an example presenting the change in mean achievement between SACMEQ I and II together with the sampling error of the difference of the means. The error bars represent two standard errors of sampling. This means that if the change were different from zero (if we can be sure 19 times out of 20, or at the 95 per cent level, that there is a difference), then the error bar will not cover the zero point indicating no change. Thus, it can be seen that in Kenya there was no significant difference. In Malawi the change was significantly different. In Mauritius the change was not significant. In Namibia, Zambia and Zanzibar the changes were significant. Thus, four out of the six countries had experienced a decline in reading scores. As the standard deviation of scores was 100, differences ranged from one tenth of a standard deviation in one country to nearly four tenths of a standard deviation in another. The question may well be asked as to why there was a decrease. In order to answer this it would be important to have measures of change in other variables. There is no confirmed information on the increase in enrolments and on the number of primary school teachers in each school that had died, for example from HIV/AIDS, and not been replaced. There were, however, measures of other changes.

An example of other variables associated with change in achievement

In *Table 3.1*, the differences between SACMEQ II and SACMEQ I for selected variables in Malawi, Namibia, Zambia and Zanzibar have been presented. Those with two asterisks indicate that differences were significant at the 95 per cent level. In this table, the actual means for SACMEQ I and II have not been presented, but only the difference of the two means together with the standard errors.

Table 3.1   Percentage and mean differences in selected variables between SACMEQ II and SACMEQ I

Variable	Malawi	Namibia	Zambia	Zanzibar
Pupil age in months	-7.1**	-11.9**	-4.9**	7.1**
Pupil sex % female	1.3	0.7	2.6	1.8
Pupil possessions	-.04	-.04**	-.07**	0.8**
Parental education	0.2	0.1	0.2	0.3
% sitting places	21.4**	-2.0	5.4**	0.2
% writing places	26.0**	1.4	32.2**	16.9**
Own reading book	-5.6	-5.9	0.7	-6.7**
Teacher age in years.	1.7	1.5	4.0**	2.2**
Teacher sex % female	1.8	-8.6	13.5*	2.4**
Teacher years' experience	0.9	0.7	3.8*	2.7**
School resources (22)	-0.42	0.10	0.15	1.7**
Class resources (8)	0.7	-0.3	0.0	0.3**

** = significantly different at the 95 per cent level.
Source: Ross *et al.*, in press.

The pupils in grade 6 were younger, with the exception of those in Zanzibar. This was presumably because the pupils were starting school at an earlier age, and this was a success from the ministries' point of view. The percentage of female pupils had increased. As a proxy measure for the financial situation of their families, pupils were asked which of 14 items they had at home. These items were: a daily newspaper, a weekly or monthly magazine, a radio, a television set, a cassette player, a video cassette recorder (VCR), a telephone, a refrigerator, a table to write on, a bicycle, a motorcycle, a car, piped water and electricity (main, generator, solar). The number of possessions owned in the home was summed up for each pupil. The lowest score possible was zero and the highest score 14. It can be seen that the pupils came from homes in which there were slightly fewer possessions in SACMEQ II than in SACMEQ I, except in Zanzibar where there was a slight increase. This is presumably because the pupils from the poorer homes were beginning to enrol in school – one of the ministries' goals.

As for school resources, pupils were asked if they sat on the floor at school or on a log or stone, or whether they sat on a chair, bench or on a seat at a desk. The latter category was taken as meaning that they had 'a sitting place'. Similarly, they were asked whether they wrote at a desk, a table or elsewhere. The former was taken to mean that they had 'a writing place'. It can be seen that either a higher percentage had their own sitting and writing places than earlier or that the situation was the same. There was no significant difference in the percentages of pupils having their own reading/textbook (i.e. not having to share) in SACMEQ I and II, except in Zanzibar where there were fewer pupils who had to share. Teachers were about the same age in SACMEQ II as in SACMEQ I, except in Zambia where they were older. There was the same proportion of female teachers, except once again in Zambia, where the proportion had increased. Years of teaching experience were the same as for age of teacher.

The school heads were asked about 22 resource items available in their school. These items were: a school library; a school hall; a staff room; a school head's office; a store room; a first-aid kit; a cafeteria; a sports area/playground; a school garden; piped water/ well or bore-hole; electricity; a radio; a tape recorder; a telephone; a fax machine; a typewriter; a duplicator; an overhead projector; a television set; a video-cassette recorder; a photocopier and a computer. In the three countries where there was a significant decrease in achievement scores, there was no significant difference in the school resources available between SACMEQ I and II. However, the actual figures for the resources in SACMEQ II were: Malawi = 4.33; Namibia = 9.91; Zambia = 6.87; and Zanzibar = 6.30. This means that the average child in Malawi was in a school with 4.33 resources. This number is very low. The average child in SACMEQ I in Malawi was in a school with 4.75 items.

Teachers were asked which of the following classroom resources were in their classrooms: a usable writing board, chalk, a wall chart of any kind, a cupboard or locker, one or more bookshelves, a classroom library, a book corner or a book box, a teacher's table and a teacher's chair – nine items in total. There were basically no differences between SACMEQ I and II. For example, in *Table 3.2* it is shown what percentage of pupils had access to the above resources in their classrooms during each of the SACMEQ studies in Malawi.

Table 3.2   Percentage of pupils whose classrooms possessed certain items in Malawi

	SACMEQ I		SACMEQ II		Difference	
Classroom resource	%	SE	%	SE	%	SE*2
Usable writing board	84.8	2.95	94.5	1.99	9.3**	7.12
Chalk	95.2	1.73	96.4	1.57	1.2	4.67
Wall chart	56.6	4.19	58.2	4.54	2.2	12.35
Cupboard	17.8	3.23	51.2	4.65	33.4**	11.32
One or more bookshelves	14.7	3.06	17.6	3.32	2.9	9.03
Classroom library	13.3	3.00	20.4	3.85	7.1	9.76
Teacher's table	40.7	4.22	47.9	4.48	7.2	12.45
Teacher's chair	43.3	4.20	50.5	4.65	7.2	12.53

** = significant at the 95 per cent level.
Source: Ross *et al.*, in press.

There were only significant differences in the percentages of pupils in classrooms with a useable writing board and a cupboard. The percentages of pupils in Malawi at the time of SACMEQ II who had classrooms with one or more bookshelves, a classroom library, a teacher's table and a teacher's chair were still low.

Finally, pupils were asked about the materials they had for use in the classroom. The figures for Malawi, Namibia, Zambia and Zanzibar have been presented in *Table 3.3*.

Table 3.3.   Percentage of pupils having various materials in SACMEQ II and SACMEQ I

Country	Exercise book	Notebook	Pencil	Eraser	Pen	Ruler
Malawi	-1.6	1.4	-13.8	-6.9	-2.6	11.3**
Namibia	0.6	-4.3	31.0**	28.7**	26.4**	20.0**
Zambia	-4.1	-11.2**	-3.1	-5.1	-5.6	2.9
Zanzibar	3.9**	18.7**	-0.3	-9.1**	-2.4**	-3.5**

** = significant difference at the 95 per cent level.
Source: Ross *et al.*, in press.

In general, there had been a deterioration in Malawi and Zanzibar, whereas in Namibia there had been an amelioration. There was not much difference between the two studies in Zambia, although the tendency was negative (i.e. a deterioration). In general, there was no clear pattern to explain why achievement should have declined in the four countries.

PISA

The PISA aims were, and still are: "PISA should, on a regular basis, provide policy-relevant information on the cumulative yield of education systems towards the end of compulsory schooling, measured in terms of the performance of students in applying knowledge and skills they have acquired in key subject areas. PISA should also collect policy-relevant information that will help policy-makers to explain differences in the performance of schools and countries. In particular, PISA was expected to address differences:

- between countries in the relationships between student level factors (such as gender and social background) and outcomes;
- in the relationships between school-level factors and outcomes across countries;
- in the proportion of variation in outcomes between (rather than within) schools, and differences in this value across countries;
- between countries in the extent to which schools moderate or increase the effects of individual-level student factors and student outcomes;
- in education systems and national contexts that are related to differences in student outcomes across countries; and
- in any or all of these relationships over time." (Source given to the author by A. Schleicher, Head of the OECD department responsible for PISA.)

The PISA group of countries opted for an age group, namely 15-year-olds, regardless of the stage they were at in the school system. By the time that PISA began, nearly all children in the OECD country education systems were in school until their sixteenth birthday. Fifteen-year-olds were spread across several grades in some systems, and more or less only across two grades in other systems. PISA is conducted once every three years. In 2000, the PISA assessment covered three domains – reading literacy, mathematical literacy and scientific literacy – with a focus on reading literacy. In PISA 2003, the focus was on mathematics, and in 2006 PISA will focus on science. This allows trends in achievement in all three areas to be plotted. Thirty-two countries took part in PISA 2000 (OECD, 2001*a*), while another 11 countries conducted the same assessment two years later (OECD, 2003*a*).

The PISA studies have been conducted with a very high level of technical expertise. This is true for all aspects of the studies. Those who undertake monitoring studies are also interested in the determinants and correlates of achievement. Three examples have been taken from PISA: The first concerns the relationship between s-e-s and achievement, the second concerns the relationship between pupil and school factors and achievement, and the third concerns the relationship between learning strategies and achievement.

An example of the relationship between s-e-s and achievement

The PISA researchers calculated the simple relationship between an individual's s-e-s and reading achievement, followed by the relationship between the school's s-e-s and reading achievement, and were then able to calculate the 'net effect' of an individual's s-e-s on reading achievement when the school (peer group) effect was accounted for (see *Figure 3.3*). An excerpt from the PISA report on this matter has been presented in *Table 3.4* below.

Table 3.4   Excerpt from PISA on the relationship between s-e-s and reading achievement

Country	Overall effect		Individual effect		School s-e-s intake effect	
	Score points	SE	Score points	SE	Score points	SE
Argentina	37.5	2.6	4.9	1.9	53.6	3.2
Australia	31.7	2.1	12.2	1.9	42.7	3.2
Belgium	38.2	2.2	6.5	1.3	61.1	2.6
Chile	39.1	1.8	7.0	1.2	42.2	1.9
Germany	45.3	2.1	3.7	1.5	63.7	2.7
Iceland	30.3	1.8	10.5	1.5	7.5	3.9
Sweden	27.1	1.5	14.1	1.5	20.6	3.2
Thailand	21.2	2.6	3.8	1.6	13.0	2.7
USA	33.5	2.7	9.9	2.0	52.8	4.3

SE = Sampling error.
Source: Excerpt from OECD, 2003*a*: Table 7.15.

The overall effect (sometimes called 'gross effect') is the increase in reading score for one unit of the socio-economic scale. This is made up from two sources: (i) the differences in s-e-s among pupils attending the same school have an impact on the differences in pupils' reading achievement within schools (the individual impact); and (ii) the differences in the average s-e-s of the pupil population in different schools have an impact on the differences in the mean results across schools (the so-called 'school s-e-s intake effect' or 'school level impact'). Take Argentina as an example. For the overall effect, it can be seen that one s-e-s unit is worth 37.5 score points in reading achievement. This can be broken down into two components: the individual (4.9 score points for one s-e-s unit) and the school intake (53.6 score points for one s-e-s unit at the school level). This means that the school s-e-s effect is much stronger than the individual effect and that, in Argentina, the school a pupil attends makes a big difference due to the social composition of the pupils in the different schools. On the other hand, in Thailand the overall effect was small (21.2 points for one s-e-s unit) and there the school s-e-s intake effect was higher than the individual effect, but neither one was strong. This means that there was some difference in achievement according to what kind of school a child attended, but that this was not as great as in other countries.

In *Figure 3.3*, the *relationships* between s-e-s and reading achievement for all countries have been presented (overall effects, individual effects and school-level effects). From this figure it can be seen that in many countries the impact of s-e-s factors on reading achievement is mainly mediated through school-level effects rather than acting simply as an individual characteristic of pupils. In general, countries with large school effects tended to have large overall (gross) effects. This indicates that when there are large school differences (sometimes called the 'social segregation effect'), then these are associated with the overall effect and hence with equity of achievement.

Some school systems want their schools or school types to be homogeneous in order to cater for specific parts of the school populations. They often have different curricula. Other school systems want their schools to be as comprehensive as possible, with all schools having the same curriculum. When choosing between these two 'philosophies', politicians need to have evidence on the effects of school differences on inequality of achievement. A monitoring study allows a country to have a quantification of the relative effects. In the next PISA study, it will be interesting to see if there have been any changes in the relative effects.

Figure 3.3 Relationships of s-e-s to reading achievement

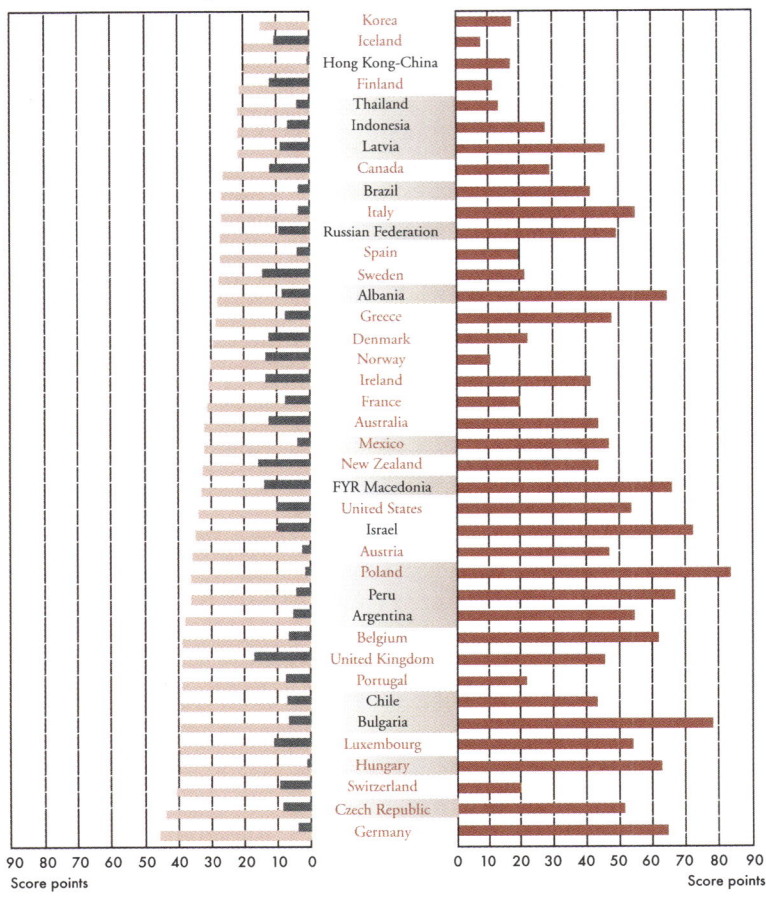

Source: OECD, 2003a: Figure 7.17.

An example of pupil and school factors associated with achievement

A second example of relationships that PISA examined was the link between several factors in schooling and reading achievement. These factors included the pupil s-e-s and the school s-e-s as well as the pupil's engagement in reading (and also the school's reading engagement), achievement pressure, a sense of belonging, cultural communication, the disciplinary climate, pupil gender, the grade level at which the pupil was enrolled, home educational resources, homework time, immigration status, family structure, books at home, the pupil-teacher relationship and class size. The results varied from country to country, but nearly all (over 70 per cent) of the between-school variance was accounted for by these variables, whereas about 25 per cent of the pupil variance was accounted for. All of the results for each country have been given in Table 7.16 in the PISA report (OEDC, 2003*a*). Readers are referred to the actual publication for the exact meaning of several of the variables. Germany and the United Kingdom have been presented below in *Table 3.5* as an example of this kind of analysis.

It can be seen that for Germany the largest effect was the s-e-s of the school (the social segregation effect). Reading engagement (both at school and individual levels) also had a strong relationship with reading achievement. Other large coefficients were pupil grade (one grade higher was worth 35 points on the reading score – nearly half a standard deviation) and immigration status (immigrants scored on average 23.5 points less than locals). In the United Kingdom, the important variables were the s-e-s (particularly at the school level), immigrant status and engagement in reading (more at the pupil level). These relationships point the school authorities to where the major problems were in the year of data collection. It is up to the authorities to initiate debate on which steps to take to deal with these major problems. How this is done in different countries would form the subject of another booklet.

Table 3.5 **Example of the relative weight of variables (regression coefficients) on reading achievement from the PISA study, 2000**

Country	Germany		United Kingdom	
	Reg. coeff.	SE	Reg. coeff.	SE
s-e-s individual	3.7	1.5	16.7	1.3
Engagement in reading	17.9	1.6	19.8	1.2
Achievement pressure	-1.5	1.2	-1.8	1.2
Sense of belonging	-0.5	1.2	-1.8	1.2
Cultural communication	-0.1	1.3	3.3	1.3
Disciplinary climate	-0.5	1.4	7.4	1.5
Pupil gender	4.3	2.3	13.8	2.3
Pupil grade	35.0	1.8	10.5	2.1
Home ed. resources	5.0	2.2	3.6	1.3
Homework time	-2.3	1.2	8.1	1.5
Immigration status	-23.5	6.3	-31.1	8.9
Family structure	-4.6	2.6	13.6	2.6
Books at home	3.9	1.1	5.6	1.0
Pupil-teacher relationship	0.6	1.2	3.2	1.3
s-e-s at school level	46.8	2.6	44.5	3.0
Reading engagement (at school level)	44.8	3.1	11.0	5.6

Source: Excerpt from OECD, 2003*a*: Table 7.15.

An example of the relationship between pupil learning approaches and achievement

Finally, a third example has been presented of the relationships between some pupil learning approaches, related factors and reading achievement (Artelt, Baumert, Julius-McElvany and Peschar, 2003). The learning approaches and related factors were:

Learning strategies:

- elaboration strategies;
- memorization strategies;
- control strategies.

Motivation:

- instrumental motivation;
- interest in reading;
- interest in mathematics;
- effort and persistence in learning.

Self-related beliefs:

- self-efficacy;
- self-concept of verbal competencies;
- self-concept of mathematical competencies;
- academic self-concept.

Self-report of social competencies:

- preference for co-operative learning;
- preference for competitive learning.

The actual questions asked for these scales have been produced in *Appendix 5*. Pupils were asked to respond by ticking, next to each item, one of the following:

disagree, disagree somewhat, agree somewhat, agree.

The following is a summary of part of the results from this study.

From the analyses it could be seen that pupils' approaches to learning had a positive effect on their achievement. Pupils who could regulate their own learning in an effective manner set realistic goals, selected learning strategies and techniques appropriate to the demands of the task at hand and maintained motivation when learning. There was a high degree of consistency within each country in the association between positive learning approaches and strong performance. Here, pupils' attitudes – their self-confidence and level of motivation – played a particularly important role alongside effective learning behaviour: The adoption of strong learning strategies. Strong attitudes were shown to be important for performance, *both* in making it more likely that pupils would adopt fruitful strategies *and* in their own right, independently of whether these strategies were actually adopted.

Pupils' approaches to learning impacted on achievement over and above the effect of family background. This was most obvious for motivational variables, such as interest in reading, and was also evident for pupils' beliefs in their own efficacy in some countries. Additionally, it could be seen that a large amount of the variability in achievement associated with pupil background was also associated with the fact that pupils from more advantaged backgrounds tended to have stronger characteristics as learners. The authors emphasized that in order to reduce social disparities in achievement it would be necessary to reduce differences in pupils' approaches to learning, which appeared to be behind much of the achievement differences.

About one fifth of the variation in pupil performance was related to the variation in approaches given in the list above. It must be assumed that the abilities assessed also depended on a range of other factors, including prior knowledge, capacity of the working memory and reasoning ability. All of these factors facilitate the process of comprehension when reading, as they free resources for deeper-level processing, meaning that new knowledge can be more easily integrated into the existing framework and hence more easily understood.

The results for each country have been presented in the PISA publication (OECD, 2003*a*). It is for the policy-makers and planners in each country to interpret the results for themselves and to decide what actions to take, if any. These results were presented in this booklet because the fact that learning strategies (and associated factors such as self-concept and interest in the subject matter) accounted for one fifth of the between-pupil variance is impressive and constitutes a major finding. It must be remembered that the PISA pupils were 15 years old and that such learning strategies will have become internalized by this age. They will therefore be very important for any future learning.

IEA

The IEA began work in 1958. It conducted a pilot study in 1960, the results of which were published in 1962 (Foshay, Thorndike, Hotyat, Pidgeon and Walker, 1962). It then conducted a first mathematics study (Husén, 1967) and went on to conduct a series of studies in several different subject matters. In the *References* section at the end of the booklet, the reader is referred to the section on IEA for a selection of publications. IEA was lucky at the outset to have some outstanding scholars who came together because they were interested in how international studies might contribute to the improvement of education in the participating countries. The standards for the conduct of such studies were high, and these standards were maintained throughout the various studies of IEA. After the six-subject study, there was a second mathematics study and then a second science study. There was also a classroom environment study, a pre-school study and a study of technology in schools. Then came a third international mathematics and science study (TIMSS), and again many of the publications have been given in the bibliography.

What are the hallmarks of IEA studies? Great care is taken in defining the subject matter and in writing and piloting the test items. The probability sampling is well conducted and where countries have not met the minimum standards they are either omitted or flagged. The data entry, data cleaning, sampling weights and standard errors of sampling are well conducted and well calculated and presented.

The reader is referred to *Chapter V* of this report to see why these aspects are so important. In the earlier IEA studies, replicated analyses of country analyses were presented as well as cross-national analyses. The replicated analyses were important in order to determine whether it was possible to generalize about the relationship to pupil and school achievement of any one or any one set of variables about the inputs to or processes in schools. In more recent years the TIMSS studies, albeit of a very high technical quality, have tended to produce books consisting of data aggregated to the national level in the first publication, and then later to produce a publication analysis, but sometimes without any coherent theme.

An example of differences among schools in achievement

One aspect of measuring educational achievement is to examine how much difference in achievement there is among schools. Many systems pride themselves that all schools are 'equal' in the sense that it does not matter to which school a child goes in the country because they will achieve equally well. A statistic known as the 'intra-class correlation' (sometimes called 'rho' or 'roh') describes the amount of variance (in this case in test scores) among schools as a proportion of all variance (i.e. among and within schools).[6] In the latest IEA reading study, known as PIRLS, the following were rhos at the grade 4 level (*Table 3.6*).

Table 3.6   Values of rhos in the PIRLS study, 2001

Country	Rho	Country	Rho
Argentina	0.418	Kuwait	0.334
Belize	0.348	Latvia	0.213
Bulgaria	0.345	Lithuania	0.214
Canada (Ontario, Quebec)	0.174	Rep. of Moldova	0.395
Colombia	0.459	Morocco	0.554

6.   It is worth mentioning that this statistic is also very important when drawing samples. Clearly, the larger the difference among schools, the more schools will be needed in the sample in order to cover all of the variance.

Table 3.6 (continued)

Country	Rho	Country	Rho
Cyprus	0.105	Netherlands	0.187
Czech Republic	0.157	New Zealand	0.250
England	0.179	Norway	0.096
France	0.161	Romania	0.351
Germany	0.141	Russian Federation	0.447
Greece	0.221	Scotland	0.179
Hong Kong (SAR)	0.295	Singapore	0.586
Hungary	0.222	Slovak Republic	0.249
Iceland	0.084	Slovenia	0.087
Islamic Republic of Iran	0.382	Sweden	0.132
Israel	0.415	Turkey	0.271
Italy	0.198	Rep. of Macedonia	0.424
		United States	0.271

SAR = Special Administrative Region.
Source: Personal communication from Pierre Foy, the sampling statistician for the PIRLS study.

For comparison's sake, it is worth also giving the rhos for the reading scores in the grade 6 SACMEQ study (*Table 3.7*), as SACMEQ involved African countries that did not take part in PIRLS.

Table 3.7   Values of rhos in SACMEQ studies, 1995-2002

SACMEQ II Country	SACMEQ I Reading	SACMEQ II Reading	Maths	Country	SACMEQ I Reading	Reading	Maths
Botswana	n/a	0.26	0.22	S. Africa	n/a	0.70	0.64
Kenya	0.42	0.45	0.38	Swaziland	n/a	0.37	0.26
Lesotho	n/a	0.39	0.30	Tanzania	n/a	0.34	0.26
Malawi	0.24	0.29	0.15	Uganda	n/a	0.57	0.65
Mauritius	0.25	0.26	0.25	Zambia	0.27	0.32	0.22
Mozambique	n/a	0.30	0.21	Zanzibar	0.17	0.25	0.33
Namibia	0.65	0.60	0.53	Zimbabwe	0.27	n/a	n/a
Seychelles	n/a	0.08	0.08	SACMEQ	0.33	0.37	0.32

n/a = not applicable because no data available for that study.
Source: Personal communication from Kenneth Ross, the Head of IIEP's team on Monitoring Educational Quality.

In the PIRLS study, the countries with the largest rhos were Singapore and Morocco. In the case of Singapore, this means that 59 per cent of all variation was due to variation among schools, and in Morocco it was 55 per cent. There were large differences among schools, and it did make a big difference to which school a child went. On the other hand, in Iceland, Slovenia and Norway it did not make much difference at all to which school a child went.

In the SACMEQ study it can be seen that Namibia, South Africa and Uganda had very high rhos. In short, in those countries – but especially South Africa – there are very large differences between schools, indicating great inequality among them. This way of looking at test scores can be very useful when determining to what extent education systems provide equality of opportunity to their children.

An example of subscores for different content areas

In the TIMSS international mathematics report (Martin, Mullis, Gonzales, Smith and Kelly, 1999), an interesting presentation was made of the relative strengths and weaknesses in different aspects of mathematics. These have been presented in *Figure 3.4*. In the TIMSS study, the researchers had arranged for sufficient items to measure various subparts of mathematics: fractions/numbers, measurement, data representation, geometry and algebra. The scores, in standard score format, are on the vertical axis. The zero point is the average score for the country. What cannot be seen from this figure are the overall differences among countries.

In the case of Australia, for example, it can be seen that for fractions and numbers, for data representation and for algebra, pupils' scores were at the average for the country, but that for geometry they were below average and for measurement above average.

It can be seen that pupils in many countries performed relatively better or worse in some content area than they did overall. For example, it can be seen that Australia performed better in measurement than on the test as a whole, but worse in geometry.

Figure 3.4 Relative performance in mathematics content in each country (TIMSS)

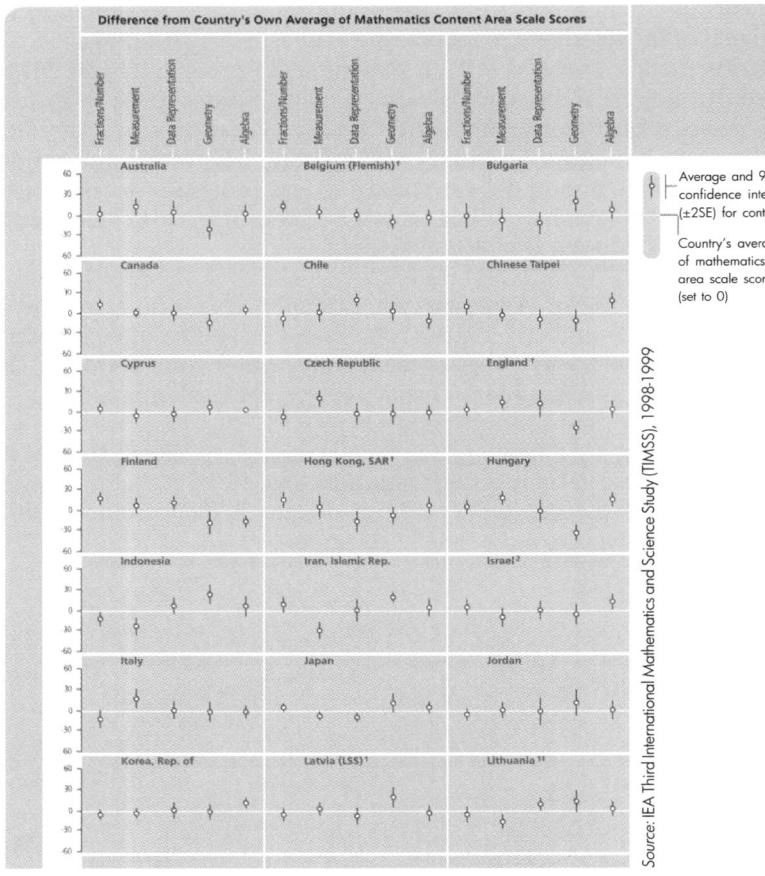

† Met guidelines for sample participation rates only after replacement schools were included (see Exhibit A.8).
1 National Desired Population does not cover all of International Desired Population (see Exhibit A.5). Because coverage falls below 65%, Latvia is annotated LSS for Latvian-Speaking Schools only.

2 National Defined Population covers less than 90 per cent of National Desired Population (see Exhibit A.5).
‡ Lithuania tested the same cohort of students as other countries, but later in 1999, at the beginning of the next school year.

Source: Martin, Mullis, Gonzales, Smith and Kelly, 1999.

Differences in performance in different content areas (the country's profile in mathematics) can be due to different emphases in the curriculum or widely used textbooks, as well as to differences in the implementation of the curriculum.

It is of interest to countries to know in which parts of mathematics pupils are stronger or weaker. Then, if they so wish, curriculum specialists can change the emphases on the various content areas of the subject matter.

An example of gender changes in reading scores

In the IEA PIRLS study (Martin, Mullis, Gonzales and Kennedy, 2003*a*), a change-of-achievement-over-time study was undertaken between 1991 and 2001. The same test items were used. In *Figure 3.5* an example of the change over time for girls and boys has been presented.

Figure 3.5   Trends in gender differences in average reading achievement (PIRLS)

Countries	2001			1991			Change in Gender Difference
	Girls Average Scale Score	Boys Average Scale Score	Difference (Absolute Value)	Girls Average Scale Score	Boys Average Scale Score	Difference (Absolute Value)	
Greece	516 (7.3) ○	499 (6.0)	18 (6.3)	476 (5.7) ○	457 (4.4)	19 (4.8)	○
Hungary	481 (4.2) ○	469 (4.2)	12 (3.2)	467 (4.4) ○	453 (4.7)	14 (4.4)	○
Iceland	517 (3.2)	508 (5.1)	9 (4.8)	501 (2.1) ○	473 (2.6)	28 (3.6)	⊙
Italy	514 (5.2)	511 (5.3)	4 (5.5)	512 (5.6) ○	495 (6.4)	17 (5.7)	○
New Zealand	520 (7.0) ○	485 (6.6)	35 (8.7)	514 (5.0) ○	485 (5.4)	29 (6.3)	○
Singapore	504 (7.9) ○	475 (8.5)	29 (4.8)	489 (3.9) ○	473 (4.5)	16 (4.3)	◉
Slovenia	508 (5.2) ○	480 (4.1)	28 (5.7)	469 (3.5) ○	447 (3.8)	22 (3.7)	○
Sweden	509 (4.3) ○	486 (4.4)	23 (4.1)	523 (4.9) ○	505 (4.8)	18 (4.6)	○
United States	517 (6.7) ○	504 (7.1)	14 (5.4)	529 (3.3) ○	513 (4.0)	16 (3.4)	○

○ Significantly higher than other gender

Increased ◉
Decreased ⊙
No Change ○

Source: Trends in IEA's reading literacy study 1991-2001

Source: Martin, Mullis, Gonzalez and Kennedy, 2003*b*: Exhibit 1.3.

The average scores for both boys and girls have been given based on the same scale for both studies. It can be seen that girls outperformed boys in all nine countries in 1991, but that by 2001, although in general girls had higher scores than boys, this was not the case in Iceland and Italy. Indeed, in Iceland the achievement difference decreased from 28 points in 1991 to 9 points in 2001, but both sexes had improved: girls by 17 points and boys by 35 score points. However, in Singapore, improved performance by girls led to an increase in the gender differences between 1991 and 2001 – from 16 to 29 score points.

This was an example of how differences between the genders can be measured over time. It is a result of planners' interest in the different countries.

IV. Criticisms of assessment studies and responses to criticisms

In this chapter, eight frequently asked questions of cross-national studies of achievement have been addressed. Some of the questions refer to international studies and some to both national and international studies.

If tests are based on a curriculum that is general to all countries, will this not result in the international studies imposing an international curriculum on all countries?

The first response is that it is highly unlikely that a national ministry of education will allow an international test to dictate its national curriculum. The second response is that the trait of reading tends to be reading, and that of mathematics tends to be mathematics. This was well illustrated in the first TIMSS study. Take, for example, the publication 'Mathematics achievement in the middle school years' (Beaton *et al.*, 1996). The authors, in Appendix B, Table B.1, compared the percentage of correct answers (or 'percentage correct') in each country according to the test as a whole (with 162 items) with the percentage correct in each country on the items said by the country to address its curriculum in mathematics (i.e. the items could be said to be covered by the curriculum. Singapore, for example, had 144 items that were covered by the Singapore curriculum). The percentage correct on the whole test and on the items covered in the curriculum was 79 in both cases. Singapore scored between 79 and 81 per cent correct on the items that other countries considered as covered in their own curricula. These ranged from 76 items in Greece to 162 in the United States. France scored 61 per cent correct on all items in the test and between 60 and 63 on the curricula of all of the other countries. Thus, it can be said that the international tests were equally fair or unfair to all countries, even if they had different curricula. In other words, any subset of items seems to measure the same as the test as a whole. This says much for the validity of the IEA international tests and for the fact that international tests do not have to affect the curricula of individual countries. Part of the table has been reproduced in *Appendix 6*.

The authors of the SACMEQ studies conducted a similar exercise with similar results. The correlation matrix of pupils' scores on the whole test and on the 'essential items' (i.e. items covered in the national curricula for both SACMEQ studies) has been presented in *Appendix 7*. Again, it can be seen that there were correlations of at least 0.99 between the essential items, the whole test and over time. This suggests very strongly that a reasonable subset of items and the whole test measure the same thing, and that countries are not disadvantaged in any way by using a carefully constructed international test. PISA obtained similar results for the reading test in 2000.

Have all competencies been measured in the international tests? Do these also include measures of children's self-esteem or of learning to live together? Could some countries downgrade the emphasis on such outcomes if international studies focus on literacy and numeracy?

In any international study it is the participating countries who decide together what will be tested (sometimes countries agree to do what other countries have done. Two years after PISA 2000, 11 countries decided to repeat the original PISA assessment). It is quite clear to the curriculum units or centres, as well as to the researchers involved, that what is tested in the international study is only one part of the whole curriculum. It is presumed that they find numeracy (or mathematics at the junior secondary level) and literacy (or reading at the junior secondary level) important.

There are two points to be made. First, in any international study there is always the possibility of having what are known as 'national option' questions. These are questions (either test items or questionnaire questions) that can be added to the international test, either in a separate instrument or at the end of the existing instruments. Thus, countries are free to add further competencies to be tested. Second, several other variables are included in the studies. In the IEA civic education studies, most of the measures were perceptual and attitudinal. In the IEA second science study, there were many attitudinal measures as well as measures of practical science. In the PISA study, there were many measures of motivation and learning strategies. This is because the countries wanted these measures to be included, and they were included and analyzed in detail (Artelt *et al.*, 2003), as has been seen earlier in this booklet.

Are students that are not used to multiple-choice questions at a disadvantage in tests that include multiple-choice format items?

Both IEA and PISA have taken a lot of trouble to ensure that nearly half of the cognitive items are not in multiple-choice format. However, items in multiple-choice format are included and the question is whether this will influence the scores of such pupils. IEA, PISA and SACMEQ have practice items at the very beginning of the tests. The test administrators are required to ensure that all pupils are *au fait* with the multiple-choice format – and, indeed, with any other format that is used (see Keeves, 1994 for a discussion of different types of tests). Once pupils are comfortable with the multiple-choice format, it is not believed that they influence the performance of those pupils who have never seen a multiple-choice formatted item before. The advantages and disadvantages of multiple-choice formatted items have been described elsewhere (Choppin, 1994). In addition to other advantages, they are also much cheaper to score than constructed-response items.

Work on the use of different item formats and achievement has been undertaken (Routitsky and Turner, 2003; Hastedt, 2004). In general, multiple-choice items tend to be easier and constructed-response (open-ended or short answer) items tend to be more difficult. Low-ability pupils tend to perform better on the multiple-choice items, while high-ability pupils tend to perform better on the constructed-response items. The rank order of countries can change very slightly if comparisons are made on either the one or the other item format.

In education systems where there is a lot of grade repetition, is testing age rather than grade fair?

IEA and SACMEQ have tested grades, and PISA has tested an age group. In the first mathematics study, IEA tested both age and grade groups. It tested an age group (e.g. all 13-year-olds, wherever they might be in the system) in order to describe, in terms of test score means and standard deviations, what an education system had done with an age cohort. However, pupils in different grades have a different curriculum and different teachers. Therefore, in order to be able to identify the relative 'effect' of different school, classroom and home practices on pupil achievement, IEA tested a grade group as well. This group was made up of the pupils enrolled in the grade where most 13-year-olds were to be found (the modal grade group). In countries where there was a lot of grade repetition, 13-year-olds could be spread across four to six grades, making it difficult to test as it was impossible to embrace in one test sufficient items to cover the range needed for the different levels of achievement involved. The TIMSS study arrived at a compromise by testing the two adjacent grades where the bulk of the age group was to be found. PISA tests all 15-year-olds in school, but even there some limits are imposed. Pupils enrolled in grades lower than grade 6 in primary school could be excluded, although countries were encouraged to include all pupils who were at least able to understand the instructions. In SACMEQ no attempt has been made to test an age group, simply as part of the age group is not in school at all and partly due to the widespread occurrence of grade repetition.

There never will be a *tabula rasa*, a clean slate or a level playing field by which to make comparisons. What is important is to get as near to one as possible, so that the general public feels that any comparisons are fair. It is a question that each study must confront and one where an explanation of the rationale for doing what the researchers did is required.

What happens if the results of a national study and tests given as part of an international study vary significantly?

If the aims of each study are the same and yet the results are different, then it is a matter of examining the technical soundness of the two studies. Questions such as the following must be raised and answered:

- Were the tests measuring exactly the same dimensions? If not, then they are hardly comparable.
- Were the excluded populations the same, and were the defined target populations the same? If not, then the two studies are not comparable.
- Were the errors about the same? If the samples were drawn to have approximately the same errors but this was not the case, then one of the studies (the one with the greater errors) will have results that are vitiated by incertitude and therefore the results cannot be trusted.
- Were the analyses appropriate? And so on.

A judgement must then be made as to which study has the most reliable results.

What is the cost of such studies?

There are two sets of costs involved in a study. The first is the set of national costs and the second the international costs. A national survey can cost between about US$20,000 and US$500,000 depending on the size of the sample, the number of instruments to be administered, entered and checked, and the form of data collection (by mail, or by data collectors going to each school for two days, requiring transport and per diem costs). Much depends on how many schools are in the sample. One unpleasant fact of life is that the more numerous the differences among schools, the more schools are needed in the sample. The minimum number of pupils per grade for each school will be about 20. In developing countries (usually poor ones), the differences among schools are greater and therefore it is those countries that need more schools in the sample.

In an international study, there are usually international costs to be paid by each national centre. These often represent US$20,000 to US$30,000 per subject per year. The total annual budget of PISA is US$3.6 million, and for IEA it is US$7.2 million.

How often should there be a national survey of a particular grade or age group?

Most researchers will agree that about once every four to five years is about right. PISA conducts national surveys every three years, which seems very frequent, but it is feared that if this were not the case the national and international teams may be disbanded. It takes a lot of work to train such teams, and to re-train them would be a terrible task. But why every four to five years? The answer is that schools tend to change (if a new head or set of teachers is appointed) during a period of about four years. At one time there was a saying in the British Inspectorate that if a school gets a poor head, the deterioration in pupil achievement will be evident in four years' time. Similarly, if it gets a good school head, the improvement will be obvious in four years' time.

What is clear is that if a country does nothing, it will never know whether the national achievement is remaining the same, improving or deteriorating.

How much influence do such studies have on decision-making on education?

This is a very difficult question to answer. In some cases, direct action is taken. The national researchers in the SACMEQ study always have a series of policy suggestions that occur in the text as particular issues (research questions), which are examined using the data from the study. The last chapter in each report summarizes the policy suggestions and proposes both a time frame for the action to be taken to fulfil the policy suggestion and a cost frame from high to low cost. Often these times and costs are worked out together with the appropriate persons in the ministries of education.

At the same time there is general agreement that research results have a 'drip effect' on public (not the general public, but the public most interested in the results) opinion and that over time the results affect how planners think about education (Husén and Kogan, 1984). In short, some results are acted upon immediately, and in other cases the effects take a generation to permeate through to improvements in the schools.

One important feature of repeat surveys is that it is possible to check if action has been taken. One example will suffice: that of improved resources. In 1990, researchers in Zimbabwe insinuated that primary school resources were at a much lower level in South Matabeleland than in other regions in Zimbabwe and therefore that school resources should be improved in that region. In 1995, a repeat survey was conducted and it was possible to see that there had been no improvement whatsoever in the level of school resources in South Matabeleland. In Namibia in 1995 there were some deficiencies in school resources, but by 2000 there had been a dramatic improvement.

It is important that a close relationship be formed between educational planners in a ministry and the researchers conducting the work. In some countries the planning unit in the ministry has a mandate to conduct the research work. This is a good development for the purpose of having action as a result of the research. However, to expect a one-to-one relationship between research results and action is unrealistic. There are costs to be considered, the relationships with the teacher unions, how parents (the electorate) would view the change, and so on.

What does beggar belief is the case in which some senior researchers (often appointed by the government) take it upon themselves to censor what is reported in research reports. They tend to delete any findings that they think the government will not like or will not like to be reported to the general public.

V. Technical standards for sample survey work in monitoring educational achievement

The aim of this chapter is to highlight ten points that readers should look for in any study in order to judge the technical soundness of the research. These ten points have come to be generally accepted as important criteria by which to judge research studies, including sample surveys used to monitor educational achievement. By applying the following questions, it should be relatively easy to judge whether a study is technically sound or not.

Some points have been marked with an asterisk (*). This denotes that these aspects of the research are particularly critical and that if the researchers have failed to do their work well in one or more of these aspects, then the results of the study are not to be trusted. It is up to readers to demand from researchers that they describe what they have done accurately and in detail.

Have the aims of the study been stated explicitly?

What were the aims of the study? Have they been clearly stated? Has the relationship of the aims to the policy and theory-oriented issues been described? Then, have the aims been operationalized into research questions? It is always troublesome to read research reports where it is unclear from the beginning which research questions the researchers were attempting to answer. Indeed, one sometimes forms the opinion that the researchers themselves were not too sure what they were trying to do. Has evidence been presented in documents or reports to show that the research questions that had been developed addressed important policy and theory-oriented issues in the country or countries concerned? (If this is not the case, then there is a danger that the research issues were the favourite topics of the researchers rather than those of the practitioners.) Is there evidence to show that the design of the study was specifically developed to allow the policy and theory-oriented issues to be answered? In some studies, great effort has been invested in the identification of the policy issues common to many systems of education. Research questions are developed to answer the policy questions, and then blank or dummy tables are developed in order to show how the answers will be reported. If this has been done, then the researchers will have reported it in their research report. Sometimes the researchers write of a conceptual model being developed. It is up to the reader to check on whether the conceptual model has resulted in specific research questions that can be answered by examining the data.

In international studies, it is sometimes stated that the interests of different systems of education are too different to be able to have a set of research questions to guide the study. In the author's experience, all countries are interested in levels of provision and attainment (of inputs, processes and outcomes), and also in the equity of these levels across administrative units, such as regions or provinces within a country as well as among schools.

The questions to pose are:

• Have the aims of the study been stated clearly and are they relevant?
• Have the research questions been developed with care?

Was the defined target population appropriate (and comparable)?

If, say, the desired target population was all pupils in second grade, the reader must ask if this grade was appropriate for the kind of questions posed about the system of education.

Where comparisons were made across countries, was like being compared with like? For example, if students in a specific grade group were being compared for their achievement, were all of the students in the grade included in the target population, or were some students excluded? It is usual that some students be 'excluded', either because they are small in number (and it would be exorbitantly expensive to collect data from them – for example, in very isolated areas) or because they are in special education schools (for example, students with visual or hearing impairments). These students are normally referred to as the 'excluded' population. It is normal to keep the number of these excluded down to less than 5 per cent of all students in the 'desired' target population. The 'defined' population is the desired population minus the excluded population. What is not acceptable is to have 2 per cent excluded in some countries and 14 per cent in others. Were the different extents of school and student level exclusions and the likely impact of these exclusions on comparisons of means and distributions across countries reported? What should make the reader extremely suspicious is when no excluded students are reported. The researcher who knows what he/she is doing will always report the extent of the excluded population, along with the reasons for such exclusion. If information has not been reported on this matter, then it is likely that no attention was paid to it and the reader therefore has no idea what is being compared with what. This is a sign of a bad study.

The same argument applies when age groups are being compared. One argument for using age groups rather than grade groups is to discover the achievement of the students born between certain dates (for example, during one calendar year). This approach seeks to examine how systems of education have coped with the education of an age cohort. Where systems have high rates of grade repetition, it is possible to have students of, say, age 13 or 14 spread across several grades. Some systems will argue that the tests are too difficult for those students who are three grades behind the others and that these students should therefore be excluded. In this case, either the tests do not have enough 'bottom' to them (i.e. there were not enough easy items to provide a sufficient distribution and the bottom end of the distribution) – in which case it can be argued that the tests are not appropriate for all of the students – or the students should be awarded zero or chance scores. One way of dealing with this problem is again to apply the rule that not more than 5 per cent of the students should be excluded.

Some of the questions to be posed are:

• Were the excluded population and the ensuing defined population described?
• Was the excluded population less than 5 per cent of the desired population?
• Were the target populations really comparable?*

Was the sampling well conducted?

The main object of sampling is to ensure that each student in the defined target population has a specified, non-zero chance of entering the sample. Was this done? As there is usually a shortfall, for various reasons, between the designed and the actual sample, it is common to calculate and use sampling weights to correct any disproportionality among sampling strata. Any study that does not report how this was done is suspect. The explanation will always be there, be it in a footnote or a technical chapter or report. The more differences there are among schools, the higher the number of schools that must be in the sample. The statistic used for describing the difference among schools is rho. Has this been mentioned?

If it is anticipated that a sector of the system or a special group of students should be studied in depth, this will require more students for that group than would normally be the case, which will have implications for the total sample size. There should also be a table in which the planned sample figures (for schools and students) and achieved sample figures (for schools and students) are presented. The response rate (proportion of schools responding multiplied by the proportion of students responding) should be greater than 0.85 (see also the section on the conduction of data collection below).

Furthermore, the population estimates derived from the samples should have a sampling error that is acceptable with respect to the policy decisions that are based on the results. Since the mid-1960s, many of the major international studies have adopted the standard of having sample designs that have the same, or better, sampling precision as a simple random sample of 400 students for educational outcome measures. This level of sampling precision provides sampling errors for results on test items (percentage correct) of no more than 2.5 per cent for one standard error, and no more than 5 per cent for two standard errors. This means, for example, that for a population estimate of 50 per cent, one can be sure, 19 times out of 20, that the true value of the 50 per cent lies between 45 and 55 per cent. As in nearly all countries the sample is a two-stage sample (first a sample of schools and then of students within schools), it is important that the standard error be calculated to take this into account. Many make the mistake of using statistical package for social sciences (SPSS) that produced a standard error that assumes that the sample was a one-stage simple random sample. This is an incorrect standard error because it has not taken into account the two-stage nature of the sample and will produce smaller standard errors than is really the case. Where differences between means were reported (say for gender or urban/rural), then differences would be found that were not really significant. A characteristic of a good study is that the correct standard error is calculated and the researchers report what they did.

The question for the reader, then, is: 'Was the sampling conducted in such a way as to yield standard errors of sampling that were acceptable for the purposes of the study?' It is usually the case that researchers who are knowledgeable in the area of sampling will have provided a detailed description of the steps of sampling and the correct sampling errors. If this information has not been provided, then there is a distinct possibility that the samples are suspect. It is also usual for the standard errors of sampling to be presented in the tables of results. If they are not there, then the reader should be wary because if, for example, the achieved sample is too small (with a large difference between the planned sample and the achieved sample), the excluded population is greater than 5 per cent or the correct rho was not known, then the calculated means and variances for any variable may be wrong.

It can sometimes be the case that the sampling has been good and that significant differences have been found. However with a large sample it is usually the case that significant differences are found. The question then arises as to whether these differences are educationally meaningful. Where a significant difference can be only worth one item on a test, then it is not educationally meaningful to report it. So, although the significant differences must be correctly calculated, the results must be interpreted with caution.

The questions to be posed about sampling are the following:

* Was the confidence limit for the sampling mentioned?*
* Was the rho used for sampling mentioned?*
* Was the response rate (schools x students) greater than 0.85?*
* Were sampling weights calculated and used?*
* Were sampling errors calculated and reported for every estimate?*
* Was care taken in the reporting about the difference between a statistically significant difference and an educationally meaningful difference?*

Were the tests well constructed and pre-tested?

It is clear that the tests must be seen to be appropriate for measuring the subject matter being tested. If they are not shown to be appropriate, valid and reliable, then the reader has every reason to be suspicious. This applies whether the test is a national or an international one.

In most cases tests are meant to measure what the students should have learned by a particular point in the school system. Occasionally, they are meant to measure what the students will need when they enter society. Whichever the case may be, it is important to prove that the tests fulfil their function.

First, it is normal to have a fairly detailed description of what is meant by reading or mathematics (or whatever the subject matter is) at the point in question in the school system. If this is missing from the research report (even as an appendix), then there are reasons to doubt the enterprise. Second, it is normal to have a test blueprint or assessment framework. This can take various forms, but is usually a grid with content on the vertical axis and cognitive behaviours on the horizontal axis. Each cell in the blueprint represents an educational objective. Again, it is normal that the blueprint be shown in the report.

Where the study aims at measuring what the students have learned to date, the test instruments must cover the intended curriculum of the country or participating countries. This normally involves a two-stage process: First, a content analysis of the curricula (via curriculum guides, textbooks, examinations, and what teachers say they teach) in the various countries; second, on the basis of the first step, the production of a national or international blueprint for the test(s). While many of the curricular objectives will be common across countries, some objectives will be common to only a subset of countries. Finally, the subject matter is often broken down into domains. In reading, this could be narrative prose, expository prose and documents, or reading for literary purposes, reading for information purposes, and so on. These domains must be specifically described.

In some cases, the study will focus on other outcomes, such as whether the pupils can read well enough to cope in society or to progress to the next grade. In these cases, exercises must first be undertaken in each country to have panels define what is required for these types of outcomes. This is a laborious process, but one which must be conducted in a convincing way.

Yet in other cases it is normal to have a hierarchical set of skills or competencies that is typical of the grade or age group being tested. Each level is described by what the students can do. An example for grade 6 from the SACMEQ study has been presented in *Table 5.1*. There were eight levels, but this covered both grade 6 students and their teachers.

Table 5.1   SACMEQ reading and mathematics skills levels

Skill level	Reading	Mathematics
Level 1	*Pre-reading*: Matches words and pictures involving concrete concepts and everyday objects, and follows short, simple, written instructions.	*Pre-numeracy*: Applies single-step addition or subtraction operations. Recognizes simple shapes. Matches numbers and pictures. Counts in whole numbers.
Level 2	*Emergent reading*: Matches words and pictures involving prepositions and abstract concepts. Uses cues (by sounding out, using simple sentence structure and familiar words) to interpret phrases by reading on.	*Emergent numeracy*: Applies a two-step addition or subtraction operation involving carrying, checking (through very basic estimation) or conversion of pictures to numbers. Estimates the length of familiar objects. Recognizes common two-dimensional shapes.
Level 3	*Basic reading*: Interprets meaning (by matching words and phrases, completing a sentence or matching adjacent words) in a short and simple text by reading on or reading back.	*Basic numeracy*: Translates verbal information (presented in a sentence, a simple graph or a table using one arithmetic operation in several repeated steps. Translates graphical information into fractions. Interprets place value of whole numbers up to thousands. Interprets simple common everyday units of measurement.
Level 4	*Reading for meaning*: Reads on or reads back in order to link and interpret information located in various parts of the text.	*Beginning numeracy*: Translates verbal or graphic information into simple arithmetic problems. Uses multiple different arithmetic operations (in the correct order) on whole numbers, fractions, and/or decimals.
Level 5	*Interpretive reading*: Reads on and reads back in order to combine and interpret information from various parts of the text in association with external information (based on recalled factual knowledge) that 'completes' and contextualizes meaning.	*Competent numeracy*: Translates verbal, graphic or tabular information into an arithmetic form in order to solve an given problem. Solves multiple-operation problems (using the correct order of arithmetic operations) involving everyday units of measurement and/or whole and mixed numbers. Converts basic measurement units from one level of measurement to another (for example metres to centimetres).

Table 5.1   (continued)

Skill level	Reading	Mathematics
Level 6	*Inferential reading*: Reads on and reads back through longer (narrative, document or expository) texts in order to combine information from various parts of the text so as to infer the writer's purpose.	*Mathematically skilled*: Solves multiple-operation problems (using the correct order of arithmetic operations) involving fractions, ratios and decimals. Translates verbal and graphic representation information into symbolic, algebraic and equation form in order to solve a given mathematical problem. Checks and estimates answers using external knowledge (not provided within the problem).
Level 7	*Analytical reading*: Locates information in longer (narrative, document or expository) texts by reading on and reading back in order to combine information from various parts of the text so as to infer the writer's personal beliefs (value systems, prejudices and/or biases).	*Problem solving*: Extracts and converts (for example, with respect to measurement units) information from tables, charts, visual and symbolic presentations in order to identify and then solve multi-step problems.
Level 8	*Critical reading*: Locates information in longer (narrative, document or expository) texts by reading on and reading back in order to combine information from various parts of the text so as to infer and evaluate what the writer has assumed about both the topic and the characteristics of the reader – such as age, knowledge, and personal beliefs (value systems, prejudices and/or biases).	*Abstract problem solving*: Identifies the nature of an unstated mathematical problem embedded within verbal or graphic information, and then translates this into symbolic, algebraic or equation form in order to solve the problem.

Source: Personal communication from Kenneth Ross, Head of IIEP's team on Monitoring Educational Quality.

In this case it is important to write items that fit each skill level.

In general, there is much less variation among countries in subjects such as reading and foreign languages than in subjects such as mathematics, history and social studies. There must, however, be agreement on the international blueprint, and this must cover the bulk of the curricula in all countries if it is the intention of the study to focus on the common contents of national curricula.

Test items must be written to cover all cells having objectives in the blueprint. The item formats must be agreed and justified. Items must be trial-tested and analyzed. Where multiple-choice items are used, the distractors must be plausible, not only in terms of content but also in their diagnostic and distracting power. Constructed-response questions requiring students to construct answers should be pre-tested to ensure that they will yield a range of responses that can be reliably scored. Where scaling is being used, there must be agreement on the substantive meaning of the scale in terms of student performance on specified tasks at specified points of the scale. There must be agreement on the appropriateness of the items and the tests must be shown to be reliable. Where there is an attempt to measure change over time, say from the last survey to the current one, then there must be sufficient common items between the two points in time to allow change to be reliably measured. Finally, items should be tested for item bias in each and every country. The psychometric properties of the test items should be similar over a sufficiently large number of countries. Where overlapping tests have to be used, it must be shown at the trial stage that the common items used to allow calibration onto the same scale fulfil their purpose. Where achievement is being measured over time, great care must be taken in the placement of the anchor items in the tests. If this is not well done, different item difficulties can ensue due to where the items were placed in the test rather than due to the items themselves. Again, the researchers will make it clear what they did in order to deal with this problem.

In some instances, hands-on performance assessment tasks may be deemed necessary to cover the full range of objectives in a subject area. The design of such tasks should take into account the (usually) limited amount of time available for testing, the need to make use of equipment that is simple and available in multiple copies and that is not beyond the resources of participating countries, and the need to yield responses that can be graded reliably across countries. Where the rotation of subtests has been undertaken, there must be proof that this was well conducted. There must, for example, be common items in the subtests, so that all items can be brought onto one scale.

Finally, there must be evidence that the tests are valid. The kinds of validity tests will have been reported if the researchers have conducted them. It is for the reader to determine whether they are convincing or not. Certainly, if the researchers have not reported them, then they have not undertaken them. In this case the reader has no idea about the validity of the tests and should be suspicious. When undertaking validity checks internationally, it is usual for the researchers to have asked the different participating countries to identify the items in the test that are part of their curriculum. The researchers then calculate a national curriculum score as well as a total test score (all items in the test, whether they are in the curriculum or not). All nations are then allocated a series of scores: the total score and then a score based on the curriculum for country A, then country B, and so on. It has been shown in various international studies that the rank order of countries does not change significantly according to which score is used. This is an indication that the test is good in the sense that it measures the outcome variable in a way that satisfies each country.

The questions to be posed for test construction are:

- Was the subject matter for the test well and convincingly described?*
- Were the domains in each subject matter well defined?*
- Were the processes used to analyze the existing curriculum or to identify the skills needed by society convincing?
- Was the item-writing process convincing?
- Were the items tried out and analyzed?*
- How was the scaling organized?*
- Were the validity checks convincing?*
- Were the test reliabilities high enough?*

Were the questionnaires and attitude scales well constructed and pre-tested?

Many believe that it is easier to construct questionnaires and attitude scales than to construct tests. They are mistaken. There is a whole technology that can be used to help with test construction. This exists to a much lesser extent for questionnaire construction. The secret for questionnaire construction (and attitude scale construction) is pilot, pilot and pilot. If no piloting occurred, then it is most likely that the measures were no good.

The questionnaire instruments must include questions to cover all of the indicators needed to answer the research questions raised at the onset of the study. Several of the indicators will be what are normally called 'derived variables' – those that are constructed from the information obtained from one or more questions. Some will be simple ratio variables while others will be factors consisting of several variables. In nearly all cases there will be a scale for an individual question or derived variable. The questions must be written in simple language easily understandable to all of the students (able and less-able) who have to answer them. All questions must then be trial-tested and analyses undertaken to ensure that the questions are providing accurate and reliable information for the indicators and derived variables. The lists of derived variables and how they have been formed are normally given in an appendix in the report, together with information on their reliabilities.

Attitude instruments, sometimes a part of the questionnaires, measure selected attitudinal dimensions. The dimensions must be described. Attitude items are normally collected through special small studies from the target population members. They too are trial-tested and analyses undertaken. Very often, about three times as many items are needed for trial testing as for the final attitude scale measure. The final scale must be shown to be reliable and valid for the purposes for which it is intended. In the description of the construction of the attitude scales, it is important to see how the researchers determined the number of options for answers.

The questions to be posed are:

- Was the process described to ensure that questions were written to cover all of the research questions for the study?*
- Were the attitude statements collected from the population for which they were intended?
- Were the questionnaires and attitude instruments subjected to several sets of piloting?*
- Were the derived variables described?*
- Where required, was the scaling of the measures described?*

In cross-national studies involving translation from a central language to others, were verifications of the translations carried out?

It is clear that all items should be translated and then checked, through a thorough verification process, to ensure that the linguistic difficulty of the item is about the same in all languages. There are elaborate procedures for doing this, and the researchers will certainly have described them if they were implemented. The verification procedure is also quite expensive. If the verification process has not been undertaken, then the reader has no idea about the comparability of the test, the questionnaire and the attitude items. In international studies questionnaire items often need adaptation from the international version to the national version. These must be thoroughly checked by the international centre. If not, one can run into problems: In one set of international questions on class size, the Spanish version asked for square metres rather than for the number of students in the class.

The main question is:

- Was a thorough verification undertaken of the translation?*

Was the data collection well conducted?

The data collection stage is crucial for any study. The object of the data collection is to test all the respondents selected in the sample and to have them complete every question in the questionnaires and all test items that they are able to answer. Normally, a manual is written for the people in charge of the data collection at the national level in each country. This manual is required so as to ensure that the data collection procedures proceed in a manner that will provide valid data under conditions that are uniform at each data collection site.

The national centre manual – sometimes called the 'NRC manual' or the 'NPM (national project manager) manual' – should cover every possible detail that must be taken into account when conducting the data collection. This involves 'school forms' and 'student forms' to ensure that the correct schools are selected, the correct students tested (and not others), and the correct teachers selected (where questionnaires or tests are being administered to teachers). A second data collection manual is usually prepared for the data collectors and details everything to be done within each selected school. A third test administration manual spells out (a) what each test administrator has to do and say during the actual testing sessions, (b) the procedures and timing for the administration of the instruments, and (c) how to parcel up the instruments and return them to a central point. There should be very few, if any, missing schools and very few missing students in the data collection. Again, the authors of the reports should give the percentage of missing schools and missing students. It is often said that not more than 10 per cent of schools should be missing from the sample and not more than 20 per cent of the students. However, since there are no completely valid procedures for dealing with missing data, these figures should be taken as absolute maximum levels.

In some studies, insufficient care is taken to ensure that there are as few non-completed questions as possible. It is essential that the research centre ensure that the tests and/or questionnaires are collected by someone who checks for this in the school before the instruments leave the school. In this way it is possible to spot questions in the questionnaires that have not been answered and to have them completed before the instruments leave the school.

In large-scale studies, it is also often the case that quality control of the actual testing is carried out. Specially trained test administrators are sent to randomly selected schools to observe the testing and verify that it is well conducted. Checks are made to ensure that the correct students are tested, that the seating in the testing room does not allow students to cheat, and so on.

As a result of the data collection, the response rate, as mentioned earlier in the section on sampling, should be at least 85 per cent (school response rate x student response rate).

The questions to be posed are:

• Were the manuals described in the research report?
• Were the tracking forms (school forms and student forms) described?
• Were the resulting response rates (without replacement schools) high enough?*
• Were there only very few missing data?*
• Was a quality control on the testing carried out?

Were the data recording, data cleaning, test scoring and sample weighting well conducted?

The data are usually recorded on computers at the national centre. Typically, the researchers provide the data entry software to be used. The researchers often undertake a double entry of 10 per cent of the instruments for verification purposes. Good data entry software provides a number of initial checks on the data that can be corrected immediately during the data entry process. Following these, all sorts of further checks are conducted in both national and international studies. Where there are several countries in the study, a common set of cleaning rules should be used. It is very difficult to compare results if each nation has used a different set of cleaning rules. There are always extra errors in data entry, no matter how good the data entry programme. By undertaking consistency checks it is possible to identify questions in the questionnaires where an error occurred on the part of the respondent. These problems are reported back to national centres;

the schools are then contacted for elucidation and the correct data sent back to the international data processing centre. The necessary changes are then made. This 'cleaning' process can take a long time, especially when there are many countries in the study. However, it should be mentioned that a data set from one country where some carelessness is evident in the data collection and/or data entry can take an inordinate amount of time to clean.

It is important for the reader to be made aware of those variables where there were so many missing data that they could not be used in the analyses. If there are many variables with more than 20 per cent missing data, then the reader should beware. Furthermore, it is important to see how the problem of missing data was tackled. There are several ways of dealing with missing data; one of them is to impute the values. Whichever approach was used, the researchers will have reported it in their report. If no mention is made of how the researchers dealt with missing data, then the reader should beware.

Where constructed-response items have been used in the test, those items will have to be scored (using a pre-established scoring guide common to all scorers and to all participating countries). Again, it is important that the scoring procedures have been reported, typically in an appendix or in a separate technical report.

Finally, in order to account for different probabilities of selection (due to shortfall in the data collection, disproportionate selection across strata, inaccurate sampling frames, missing data, etc.), sampling weights must be calculated. As there is nearly always a shortfall in survey studies, sampling weights are needed. Either there will be a description in the report about how the weights were calculated, or (but only in exceptional circumstances) there will be a description and justification of why sampling weights were not required. If there is no description of how sampling weights were calculated, it is very likely that they were not used and therefore the estimate of the means and variances of variables will be wrong.

The questions to be posed are:

- Was a data entry programme used that included consistency checks?*
- Were further checks carried out?*
- Were there many variables with more than 20 per cent missing data?
- Were sampling weights calculated and used?*

Were the data analyses well conducted?

In all reports there are usually some univariate analyses and some multivariate analyses. Although the analyses must fit the research questions, most issues are sufficiently complex to warrant more than only univariate analyses.

Some of the analyses will be simple, and others complex. It is normal for a study to have a set of dummy tables produced at the onset of the study. These dummy tables cover the research questions posed. The analyses will have been undertaken to complete the tables. If the reader is not experienced in data analysis, it is usually wise to have experts advise him or her on the appropriateness of the analyses for the questions posed.

Some examples of 'inappropriate' analyses often encountered in poor studies might be of use to readers. It can happen that the researchers report a mean score for a cell on a test blueprint (an aspect of achievement) despite the fact that the number of items per cell was insufficient to derive a separate scale. It can also happen that the researchers comment on a zero-order correlation without considering and testing if it would be non-significant if other variables, such as the s-e-s of the students or school location (rural/urban), were controlled. Another example would be undertaking multivariate analyses between schools using 100 variables when there are only 150 schools (normally, in a case like this, one would need at least six times as many schools than variables.)

Where new constructs (or factors) and scales have been produced during the data analyses, it is important that they be described in the report.

There are also errors in interpretation that occur in poor studies. Sometimes the authors of the research reports exhibit a lack of caution when they forget that correlations do not necessarily signify causation; or when they forget that the responses to perceptual questions do not necessarily depict what is actually the case (for example, teachers' perceptions of the goals of the school collected through a teacher questionnaire).

As mentioned earlier, it is important that each estimate be accompanied by a standard error of sampling. There are now good programmes for the calculation of standard errors and it is reasonable to expect that every estimate should be accompanied in the tables and figures by the standard error of sampling. If a report does not include these, then the reader should be suspicious as to whether the researchers know what they are doing.

Some of the questions to be posed are:

- In reporting test scores (either total scores or subscores), were sufficient items used to create the score? If not, then the reader should be suspicious as to whether the researchers knew what they were doing.*
- Were the appropriate variables taken into account when examining relationships between variables?*
- Have the standard errors of sampling been reported for every estimate in the report?*

Were the reports well written?

The reports should be clearly written and deal with each of the policy issues in turn. The source of the data under discussion should always be clear, as should arguments concerning the interpretation of the analyses. It should be made clear that in some studies the major univariate results are reported first and major clusters of research questions are reported in separate reports.

It is important that the researchers obtain feedback on their reports before the reports are finalized. In part, this is from other researchers, but also from the intended users of the results in the report as well as from concerned persons such as school heads and teachers. Where the main users of the results will be ministries of education, it helps a great deal if the researchers have discussed their recommendations with those responsible in the ministries of education before publication. Again, if the researchers have done this, they will also have described the process. It is also useful to ministries of education if the researchers cluster their recommendations (policy suggestions) drawn from the study results not only by theme but also by cost (low, medium and high) and by length of implementation (short, medium and long term).

Finally, it is normal for the researchers to make the data set(s) available as an archive so that others can analyze the data themselves in order to check the veracity of the statements that the researchers have made and also to explore the data to answer other questions that might be asked about the data. It is very important that the archives be made available very soon after (or even at the same time as) publication and in a format that is user friendly.

VI. Conclusion and some implications for educational planners

It will have been seen from the foregoing that it is imperative to conduct studies such as those mentioned if the authorities wish to know about achievement in their systems of education. Just as management systems collect data at regular intervals on inputs to schools and enrolments, so the authorities will need to collect data on achievement at regular intervals.

In many countries, those in charge of the management of education systems turn to the planning divisions or units to collect the achievement data. In this case, either the heads of the planning divisions have to ensure that the members of the division have the necessary skills (and it takes quite a long time to learn them), or they must outsource it. In order to outsource the work, it will be incumbent on the head of planning to ensure that one or two members of the division are well versed in the kinds of technical matters mentioned in *Chapter V*. If they are not well versed, then they will run the risk of not selecting an adequate institution to which to outsource the work. It may be that there is a national institute of educational research, but it would be wise to ensure that this institute does in fact have the required skills and experience. In this sense, the training of key staff is essential.

There are various other points for the planners to consider.

Staffing

If the work has to be done in the planning unit, then the head of planning must ensure that he or she has a skeleton staff. One common staffing plan has been given as an example.

1.   One head of monitoring (full time). This person should have proven competence in flexible administration as well as in instrument construction.
2.   One planning officer (full time) versed in statistical analysis (using SPSS and SAS) and probability sampling. This person should also have practical experience of a data entry programme such as WINDEM.

Both of the above should be good at interpreting data analyses and writing up the results.

3.   Several part-time officers (five to seven) to assist with instrument construction. Some of these will probably come from the curriculum centre.
4.   Several people to enter and clean the data. These will only be required twice – once at the pilot stage and once at the main data collection stage.

The head of monitoring will need to ensure that the requisite machines and rooms (not forgetting a storage room for the instruments when they are returned from the schools) are available.

Even if the work is outsourced, there are two stages in the work where the planning unit must be very busy: at the beginning of the whole process, and again at the end. At the very beginning, the planning unit will need to liaise with all of the departments in the ministry in order to elicit the kinds of research questions they would like to have answered by the research. These must be precisely formulated, so that they can be used to determine all of the measures to be used in the research. At the end of the research, when the answers to the research questions are known, the planning unit will need to develop the policy recommendations emanating from the research in conjunction with the relevant people in the ministry's departments.

If it is an international study, there is still a need to have a national report.

It is for the planning division to ensure that there is a national report. It is rarely sufficient for a country to have only the international report published. Indeed, many countries will have added special national option variables, and these will not be analyzed internationally but rather nationally for inclusion in the national reports. This is a simple point, but one that needs to be made nonetheless.

Linking of EMIS databases to sample survey databases

Many countries have an educational management information system whereby yearly audits of schools are conducted, collecting data on some 20 to 60 variables in each school. Where such data exist, it would seem unnecessary to collect the data again in a sample survey. There should be ways and means of merging the data from one database into another. This requires that the school ID data be the same for both. In some countries this is the case, but in others it is not. It is up to the planners to devise an ID system for schools within districts and within regions in the country so that the ID system can also be used by other surveys.

Some political dangers to be considered

Examples have been given in the booklet of achievement being reported in terms of minimum and desirable levels being obtained. It is a brave ministry of education that allows these standards to be set before the test is even administered. This involves panels of subject-matter specialists (and sometimes others) deciding on which items (or percentage of subset of items) should be used to designate minimum and desirable levels. What happens if only 50 per cent of pupils reach the minimum level? It might be politically embarrassing. Nevertheless, many ministries want exactly this kind of information. In some cases they inform the public, and in others they do not do so, but who should decide on this?

What happens if a country that has participated in an international study comes first or last in the international rank order by score? If the country is first, the danger is that the powers-that-be will take no action at all because they say that all is well. If the country comes last it might be humiliating. The minister might wonder if it is worth spending all of the money required to run a monitoring study just to be last. However, some ministries of countries that have been last have welcomed this fact and tried to improve. After all, as they say: the only way to go is up! Luckily, it is not the rank order that is important (although some argue that it is always of interest to see how the country is doing compared with other selected countries), but rather the spreads of achievement scores among pupils, schools and regions within the country that are important. Equally important are the relationships among variables and knowing what to do to improve the current form and content of schooling. Moreover, not all countries are good in all subject areas.

The importance of malleable variables

Not all of the factors affecting achievement will be manipulable or malleable, but many will be. It is important to decide which are malleable and the most easily changed by ministries of education. Even where it is shown that pupils whose parents take an active interest in their children's schooling perform better, it is too easy to shrug off the finding with comments such as: 'Ah well, that is the business of the home. We, the Ministry, can't do anything there'. And yet there have been successful programmes (often called intervention programmes) where the schools organize programmes in the schools that are attended by mothers and result in changes in parental behaviour in the home (for examples see Norisah, Naimah, Abu and Solehan, 1982; and Kellaghan, Sloane, Alvarez and Bloom, 1993).

It is for the planners to examine the results of the study, identify where improvements in the system can be made and discuss with the researchers and heads of divisions within the ministry to ensure that very practical suggestions (with cost and length of time for implementation estimates) are included at the end of the national report. In some cases, however, it will be sufficient to highlight the finding (and the problems it raises) and then encourage public debate on what the solution might be.

Dissemination

Dissemination of information about a monitoring study before it takes place, and dissemination of the results of the study after the study has been completed, require careful planning. Much will depend on the 'freedom of information' climate in the country.

For the dissemination of information about a study, it is sufficient for the ministry to inform the selected schools that they have been selected and they will participate. In other countries the researchers must convince various people. For example, in Germany it is incumbent on the researchers to obtain permission from five groups:

* the provincial or regional education office;
* the school heads;
* the teacher body in each school (and this can involve the teacher unions);
* the parent council in the school; and
* the pupil body.

If, say, 200 schools have been drawn in the sample, this implies 800 permissions plus the number of regional directors. In such circumstances, the monitoring project must employ a person whose task it is to convince them that the expected results will lead to improvements in the system and that their participation is therefore worthwhile.

Depending on the degree of decentralization in a country, the results will be of more interest to the national, provincial or even the district level. The utility of these different levels will depend on the sample design. Most samples are drawn to yield accurate information at the national level. If accurate information is required for each province, then this will increase the number of schools in the sample several-fold. Thus, the levels at which accurate information is required must be planned at the very beginning of a study.

It is common for the researchers to provide feedback to the schools on the test results (separately for each subject area tested) where each pupil's score is provided. An average score for the school is also provided together with the average score for similar schools (either in terms of similar school type or similar s-e-s intake of pupils) and an average score for the nation.

There will be a plan for the kinds of reports required for different audiences. The planners will need to decide on how many reports should be written. These might include:

- an overall research report;
- a report written for senior members of the ministry;
- a report for Parliament;
- a report for the general public;
- a report for the media;
- a report for school heads and teachers; and so on.

It is also common for some ministries to arrange meetings of school heads and teachers in the different regions of the country to discuss the results.

A final remark

Despite the dangers and all the skills needed to conduct studies of this kind, an increasing number of countries require the kind of information that such studies yield. It is clear that it is better to have this kind of information as one input to the decision-making process than not to have it. However, it is essential that the ministry take the initial step of deciding what it wants to know (the formulation of the research questions) and then ensure that the study is conducted to a high standard of quality, so that the results can be trusted. Finally, great care must be taken in the interpretation of the results and suggestions for improving the system that flow from the study. Once a monitoring team has been trained, great care should be taken to preserve the team and not let it be disbanded. Training is a must for key personnel in the planning divisions of the ministries.

References

General

Choppin, B.H. 1994. "Objective tests in measurement". In: T. Husén and T.N. Postlethwaite. (Eds.), *International encyclopedia of education* (2nd edition). Oxford: Pergamon Press.

Coleman, J.S.; Campbell, E.Q.; Hobson, C.J.; McPartland, J.; Mood, A.M.; Weinfeld, F.D.; York, R.L. 1966. *Equality of educational opportunity.* Salem, New Hampshire: Ayer and Co. Available at http://www.garfield.library.upenn.edu/classics1979/A1979HZ27500001.pdf.

De Landsheere, G. 1994. *Le pilotage des systèmes d'éducation.* Brussels: De Boeck-Wasmael.

Douglas, J.W.B. 1964. *The home and the school: A study of ability and attainment in the primary schools.* London: MacGibbon and Kee.

Fägerlind, I. 1975. *Formal education and adult earnings: A longitudinal study on the economic benefits of education.* Stockholm: Almqvist and Wiksell.

Foshay, A.W. (Ed.). 1962. *Educational achievement of thirteen-year-olds in twelve countries.* Hamburg: UNESCO Institute for Education.

Hastedt, D. 2004. "Differences between multiple-choice and constructed response items in PIRLS 2001". In: C. Papanastasiou (Ed.), *Proceedings of the IEA International Research Conference 2004. PIRLS, Vol 3.* Nicosia: University of Cyprus Press.

Husén, T.; Kogan, M. (Eds.). 1984. *Educational research and policy. How do they relate?* Oxford: Pergamon Press.

Keeves, J.P. 1994. "Tests: Different types". In: T. Husén and T.N. Postlethwaite (Eds.), *International encyclopedia of education* (2nd edition). Oxford: Pergamon Press.

Kellaghan, T.; Greaney, V. 2001. *Using assessment to improve the quality of education*. Fundamentals of educational planning series, No. 71. Paris: IIEP-UNESCO.

Kellaghan, T.; Sloane, K.; Alvarez, B.; Bloom, B.S. 1993. *The home environment and school learning*. San Francisco: Jossey-Bass Publishers.

Norisah bt Atan; Naimah bt Haji Abdullah; Abu Bakar Nordin; Solehan bin Remot. 1982. "Remedial reading support program for children in grade 2 Malaysia". In: *Evaluation in Education, 6*, 137-160. Oxford: Pergamon Press.

Peaker, G.F. 1971. *The Plowden children four years later*. Slough: NFER.

Pidgeon, D.A. 1958. "A comparative study of basic attainments". In: *Educational Research, 1*(1), 50-68.

Routitsky, A.; Turner, R. 2003. *Item format types and their influence on cross-national comparisons of student performance*. Paper presented at the Annual Meeting of the American Educational Research Association (AERA), in Chicago, USA, April 2003.

Scottish Council for Research in Education. 1949. *The trend in Scottish intelligence: A comparison of the 1947 and 1932 surveys of the intelligence of eleven-year-old pupils*. London: University of London Press.

Tyler, R.W. 1985. "National Assessment of Educational Progress (NAEP)". In: T. Husén and T.N. Postlethwaite (Eds.), *The international encyclopedia of education* (1st edition). Oxford: Pergamon Press.

UNESCO Institute for Statistics. 2004. *Global education digest 2004: Comparing education statistics across the world.* Montreal: UNESCO Institute for Statistics.

Ministry of Education and Training. (in press). *The quality of education at the end of primary school. Vietnam, 2001. The levels and determinants of grade 5 reading and mathematics achievement.* Vietnam: Ministry of Education and Training.

PISA

Artelt, C.; Baumert, J.; Julius-McElvany, N.; Peschar, J. 2003. *Learners for life: Student approaches to learning. Results from PISA 2000.* Paris: OECD.

Döbert, H.; Klieme, E.; Sroka, W. (Eds.). 2004. *Conditions of school performance in seven countries. A quest for understanding the international variation of PISA results.* Münster: Waxmann.

OECD. 2001*a*. *Knowledge and skills for life. First results from PISA 2000.* Paris: OECD.

OECD (Eds. R. Adams and M. Wu). 2001*b*. *PISA 2000 technical report.* Paris: OECD.

OECD. 2002. *Reading for change. Performance and engagement across countries.* Paris: OECD.

OECD. 2003*a*. *Literacy skills for the world of tomorrow. Further results from PISA 2000.* Paris: OECD.
Available at http://www.oecd.org/document/49/
0,2340,en_2649_37455_2997873_119699_1_1_37455,00.html

OECD. 2003*b*. *Student engagement at school: A sense of belonging and participation. Results from PISA 2000*. Paris: OECD.

IEA (some selected publications only)

Anderson, L.W.; Ryan, D.W.; Shapiro, R.J. (Eds.). 1989. *The IEA classroom environment study. International studies in educational achievement, Vol. 2*. Oxford: Pergamon Press.

Beaton, A.E.; Martin, M.O.; Mullis, I.V.S.; Gonzales, E.J.; Smith, T.A.; Kelly, D.L. 1996. *Science achievement in the middle school years: IEA's TIMSS*. Chestnut Hill, MA: Boston College.

Beaton, A.E.; Mullis, I.V.S.; Martin, M.O.; Gonzales, E.J.; Kelly, D.L.; Smith, T.A. 1996. *Mathematics achievement in the middle school years: IEA's TIMSS*. Chestnut Hill, MA: Boston College.

Burstein, L. (Ed.). 1993. *The IEA study of mathematics, Vol. 3. Student growth and classroom practices*. Oxford: Pergamon Press.

Campbell, Jr.; Kelly, D.L.; Mullis, I.V.S.; Martin, M.O.; Sainsbury, M. 2001. *Framework and specifications for PIRLS assessment 2001*, 2nd edition. Boston: IEA.

Carroll, J.B. 1975. *The teaching of French as a foreign language in eight countries. International studies in evaluation, Vol. 5*. New York: Wiley.

Comber, L.C.; Keeves, J.P. 1973. *Science education in nineteen countries: An empirical study. International studies in evaluation, Vol. 1*. New York: Wiley.

Degenhart, R.E. 1990. *Thirty years of international research: An annotated bibliography of IEA publications (1960-1990)*. The Hague: IEA.

Elley, W.B. (Ed.). 1992. *The IEA study of reading literacy: Achievement and instruction in thirty-two school systems. International studies in educational achievement.* Oxford: Pergamon.

Foshay, A.W.; Thorndike, R.L.; Hotyat, F.; Pidgeon, D.A.; Walker, D.A. (Ed.). 1962. *Educational achievement of thirteen-year-olds in twelve countries.* Hamburg: UNESCO Institute for Education.

Garden, R.A.; Robitaille, D.F. 1989. *The IEA study of mathematics II: Contexts and outcomes of school mathematics.* Oxford: Pergamon Press.

Gorman, T.P.; Purves, A.C.; Degenhart, R.E. (Eds.). 1988 *The IEA study of written composition I: The international writing tasks and scoring scales.* Oxford: Pergamon Press.

Husén, T. (Ed.). 1967. *International study of achievement in mathematics: A comparison of twelve countries, Vols. 1-2.* Stockholm: Almqvist and Wiksell.

Keeves, J.P. (Ed.). 1992. *The IEA study of science: Changes in science education and achievement: 1970 to 1984.* Oxford: Pergamon Press. (See also Chapter 9 in this book by J.P. Keeves and A. Schleicher on "Changes in science achievement 1970-84").

Keeves, J.P. 1995. *The world of school learning: Selected key findings from 35 years of IEA research.* The Hague: IEA.

Keeves, J.P. 2001. "Comparative research in education: IEA studies". In: N.J. Smelser and P.B. Baltes (Eds.), *International encyclopedia of the social and behavioral sciences* (pp. 2421-2427). Oxford: Pergamon Press.

Lewis, E.G.; Massad, C.E. 1975. *The teaching of English as a foreign language in ten countries. International studies in evaluation, Vol. 4.* Stockholm: Almqvist and Wiksell.

Martin, M.O.; Kelly, D.L. (Eds.). 1996. *TIMSS technical report: Vol. 1. Design and development*. Chestnut Hill, MA: Boston College.

Martin, M.O.; Kelly, D.L. (Eds.). 1997. *TIMSS technical report. Vol. 2. Implementation and analysis, primary and middle school years*. Chestnut Hill, MA: Boston College.

Martin, M.O.; Kelly, D.L. (Eds.). 1998. *TIMSS technical report: Vol. 3. Implementation and analysis, final year of secondary school*. Chestnut Hill, MA: Boston College.

Martin, M.O.; Mullis, I.V.S. (Eds.). 1996. *TIMSS: Quality assurance in data collection*. Chestnut Hill, MA: Boston College.

Martin, M.O.; Mullis, I.V.S.; Beaton, A.E.; Gonzales, E.J.; Smith, T.A.; Kelly, D.L. 1997. *Science achievement in the primary school years: IEA's TIMSS*. Chestnut Hill, MA: Boston College.

Martin, M.O.; Mullis, I.V.S.; Gonzales, E.J.; Smith, T.A.; Kelly, D.L. 1999. *School context for learning and instruction in IEA's Third International Mathematics and Science Study (TIMSS)*. Chestnut Hill, MA: Boston College.

Martin, M.O.; Mullis, I.V.S.; Gonzales, E.J.; Kennedy, A.M. 2003*a*. *PIRLS 2001 international report: IEA's study of reading literacy achievement in primary schools*. Boston: IEA.

Martin, M.O.; Mullis, I.V.S.; Gonzales, E.J.; Kennedy, A.M. 2003*b*. *Trends in children's reading literacy achievement, 1991-2001*. Boston: IEA.

Martin, M.O.; Mullis, I.V.S.; Gregory, K.D.; Hoyle, C.; Shen, C. 2001. *Effective schools in science and mathematics*. Chestnut Hill, MA: Boston College.

Martin, M.O.; Mullis, I.V.S.; Kennedy, A.M. 2003. *PIRLS (2001) technical report*. Boston: IEA.

Martin, M.O.; Rust, K.; Adams, R.J. (Eds.). 1999. *Technical standards for IEA studies*. Amsterdam: IEA Secretariat.

Mullis, I.V.S.; Martin, M.O.; Beaton, A.E.; Gonzales, E.J.; Kelly, D.L.; Smith, T.A. 1998. *Mathematics and science achievement in the final year of secondary school: IEA's TIMSS*. Chestnut Hill, MA: Boston College.

Mullis, I.V.S.; Martin, M.O.; Fierros, E.G.; Goldberg, A.L.; Stemler, S.E. 2000. *Gender differences in achievement: IEA's Third International Mathematics and Science Study (TIMSS)*. Chestnut Hill, MA: Boston College.

Mullis, I.V.S.; Martin, M.O.; Kennedy, A.M.; Flaherty, C.L. (Eds.). 2002. *PIRLS 2001 Encyclopedia: A reference guide to reading education in the countries participating in IEA's Progress in International Reading Literacy Study (PIRLS)*. Boston: IEA.

Olmsted, P.P.; Montie, J. 2001. *Early childhood settings in 15 countries: What are their structural characteristics?* Ypsilanti, MI: High/Scope Press.

Olmsted, P.P.; Weikart, D.P. 1989. *How nations serve young children: Profiles of child care and education in 14 countries*. Ypsilanti, MI: High/Scope Press.

Olmsted, P.P.; Weikart, D.P. 1994. *Families speak: Early care and education in 11 countries*. Ypsilanti, MI: High/Scope Press.

Passow, A.H.; Noah, H.J.; Eckstein, M.A.; Mallea, J.R. 1976. *The national case study: An empirical comparative study of twenty-one educational systems. International studies in evaluation, Vol. 7*. Stockholm: Almqvist and Wiksell.

Peaker, G.F. 1975. *An empirical study of education in twenty-one countries: A technical report. International studies in evaluation, Vol. 8*. Stockholm: Almqvist and Wiksell.

Pelgrum, W.J.; Plomp, T. 1991. *The use of computers in education worldwide: Results from the IEA 'Computers in Education' survey in nineteen educational systems.* Oxford: Pergamon Press.

Postlethwaite, T.N.; Wiley, D.E. 1992. *The IEA study of science II: Science achievement in twenty-three countries.* Oxford: Pergamon Press.

Purves, A.C. 1973. *Literature education in ten countries: An empirical study. International studies in evaluation, Vol. 2.* Stockholm: Almqvist and Wiksell.

Purves, A.C. (Ed.). 1992. *The IEA study of written composition II: Education and performance in fourteen countries.* Oxford: Pergamon Press.

Robitaille, D.F.; Beaton, A.E. (Eds.). 2002. *Secondary analysis of the TIMSS data.* Dordrecht: Kluwer.

Robitaille, D.F.; Beaton, A.E.; Plomp, T. (Eds.). 2000. *The impact of TIMSS on the teaching and learning of mathematics and science.* Vancouver, BC: Pacific Educational Press.

Rosier, M.J.; Keeves, J.P. 1991. *The IEA study of science I: science education and curricula in twenty-three countries.* Oxford: Pergamon Press.

Stevenson, H.W.; Lummis, M.; Lee, S.-Y.; Stigler, L.W. 1990. *Making the grade in mathematics: Elementary school mathematics in the United States, Taiwan, and Japan.* Reston, Virginia: National Council of Teachers of Mathematics.

Thorndike, R.L. 1962. "International comparison of the achievement of thirteen-year-olds". In: A.W. Foshay (Ed.). 1962. *Educational achievement of thirteen-year-olds in twelve countries.* Hamburg: UNESCO Institute for Education.

Thorndike, R.L. 1973. *Reading comprehension education in fifteen countries: An empirical study. International studies in evaluation, Vol. 3.* Stockholm: Almqvist and Wiksell.

Torney, J.V.; Oppenheim, A.N.; Farnen, R.F. 1976. *Civic education in ten countries: An empirical study. International studies in evaluation, Vol. 6.* Stockholm: Almqvist and Wiksell.

Torney-Purta, J.; Lehmann, R.; Oswald, H.; Schulz, W. 2001. *Citizenship and education in twenty-eight countries: civic knowledge and engagement at age fourteen.* Delft: IEA.

Torney-Purta, J.; Schwille, J.; Amadeo, J.-A. (Eds.). 1999. *Civic education across countries: twenty-four national case studies for the IEA Civic Education Project.* Delft: IEA.

Travers, K.J.; Westbury, I. 1989. *The IEA study of mathematics I: international analysis of mathematics curricula.* Oxford: Pergamon Press.

Walker, D.A. 1976. *The IEA six-subject survey: an empirical study of education in twenty-one countries. International studies in evaluation, Vol. 9.* Stockholm: Almqvist and Wiksell.

Weikart, D.P. 1999. *What should young children learn? Teacher and parent views in 15 countries.* Ypsilanti: MI: High/Scope Press.

Weikart, D.P.; Olmsted, P.P.; Montie, J. 2003. *World of preschool experience: observation in 15 countries.* Ypsilanti, MI: High/Scope Press.

SACMEQ

Kulpoo, D. 1998. *The quality of education: some policy suggestions based on a survey of schools – Mauritius. SACMEQ Policy Research: Report No. 1.* Paris: IIEP-UNESCO.

Machingaidze, T.; Pfukani, P.; Shumba, S. 1998. *The quality of education: some policy suggestions based on a survey of schools – Zimbabwe. SACMEQ Policy Research: Report No. 3*. Paris: IIEP-UNESCO.

Milner, G.; Chimombo, J.; Banda, T.; Mchikoma, C. 2001. *The quality of education: some policy suggestions based on a survey of schools – Malawi. SACMEQ Policy Research: Report No. 7.* Paris: IIEP-UNESCO.

Nassor, S.; Mohammad, K. 1998. *The quality of education: some policy suggestions based on a survey of schools – Zanzibar. SACMEQ Policy Research: Report No. 4.* Paris: IIEP-UNESCO.

Nkamba, M.; Kanyika, J. 1998. *The quality of education: some policy suggestions based on a survey of schools – Zambia. SACMEQ Policy Research: Report No. 5.* Paris: IIEP-UNESCO.

Nzomo, J.; Kariuki, M.; Guantai, L. 2001. *The quality of education: some policy suggestions based on a survey of schools – Kenya. SACMEQ Policy Research: Report No. 6.* Paris: IIEP-UNESCO.

Ross, K. (Ed.). In press. *The SACMEQ II study in Kenya.*

Ross, K.; Saito, M.; Dolata, S.; Ikeda, M. In press. *SACMEQ data archive.* Paris: IIEP-UNESCO.

Saito, M. 2004. "Gender equality in reading and mathematics: Reflecting on EFA Goal 5". In: *IIEP Newsletter*, pp.8-9. April-June, 2004.

Voigts, F. 1998. *The quality of education: some policy suggestions based on a survey of schools – Namibia.* Paris: IIEP-UNESCO.

Appendices

Appendix 1. General research questions from the Vietnam study

Each of the questions below was subdivided into many specific research questions. These general questions have been listed simply to give a flavour of the kinds of questions asked in the Vietnam study.

Policy questions related to educational inputs

a) *What were the characteristics of grade 5 pupils?*
b) *What were the characteristics of grade 5 teachers?*
c) *What were the teaching conditions in grade 5 classrooms and in primary schools?*
d) *What aspects of the teaching function designed to improve the quality of education were in place?*
e) *What was the general condition of school buildings?*
f) *What level of access did pupils have to textbooks and library books?*

Specific questions relating to a comparison of reality in the schools and the benchmarks set by the MOET and the Fundamental School Quality Levels

Were the following benchmarks met? (total school enrolment, class size, classroom space, staffing ratio, sitting places, writing places, chalkboard, classroom furniture, classroom supplies, academic qualification of school heads, professional qualification of school heads, etc.).

Have the educational inputs to schools been allocated in an equitable fashion?

a) *What was the equity of material resource inputs among regions, among provinces and among schools within provinces?*
b) *What was the equity of human resource inputs among provinces and among schools within provinces?*
c) *How different was pupil achievement among regions, among provinces and among schools within provinces?*

Which were the variables most associated with the difference between the most effective and least effective schools?

Which variables were most associated with achievement?

Appendix 2. Vietnam grade 5: Percentages and sampling errors of pupils at different skill levels in reading in each province and region

Region	Province	Reading Skill Levels (pupil)											
		Level 1		Level 2		Level 3		Level 4		Level 5		Level 6	
		%	SE	%	SE	%	SE	%	SE	%	SE	%	SE
Red River Delta	Ha Noi	0.9	0.38	5.4	1.31	15.1	1.99	18.9	1.73	33.5	2.48	26.2	2.83
	Hai Phong	2.2	0.62	9.0	1.35	23.5	2.25	20.4	1.82	27.9	2.42	17.0	3.06
	Ha Tay	2.7	0.69	11.5	1.66	21.0	2.56	21.8	2.34	27.2	3.10	15.8	3.29
	Hai Duong	1.6	0.43	8.0	1.52	19.1	2.24	18.4	1.98	28.4	2.90	24.5	4.31
	Hung Yen	2.1	0.72	7.1	1.40	16.0	2.42	21.4	1.95	32.9	3.11	20.4	3.52
	Ha Nam	4.0	0.92	15.2	1.61	26.4	2.30	23.6	2.38	23.1	2.35	7.8	1.80
	Nam Dinh	0.9	0.27	6.1	1.18	15.5	1.94	21.5	1.94	38.9	2.68	17.2	2.79
	Thai Binh	0.6	0.25	3.8	0.83	16.3	2.13	20.6	2.13	34.2	2.71	24.6	3.87
	Ninh Binh	4.6	1.08	16.6	1.81	32.4	1.93	24.1	1.74	16.7	1.78	5.6	1.55
North-East	Ha Giang	7.5	1.66	22.1	3.23	27.4	3.06	18.7	2.97	18.5	3.07	5.7	2.09
	Cao Bang	14.4	3.16	22.4	3.28	23.4	3.11	16.2	2.61	14.9	3.10	8.7	3.04
	Lao Cai	1.4	0.78	6.7	1.68	15.3	2.18	22.7	2.90	38.2	3.59	15.7	3.40
	Bac Kan	8.2	2.02	21.5	2.77	26.3	2.67	15.5	2.25	18.7	3.09	9.9	3.07
	Lang Son	11.0	2.20	26.2	2.87	22.2	2.32	18.2	2.45	16.9	2.98	5.6	1.46
	Tuyen Quang	12.5	2.26	24.9	2.71	24.2	2.56	18.7	2.23	15.7	2.71	3.9	1.30
	Yen Bai	11.4	2.27	20.9	2.40	23.1	2.24	17.8	2.15	14.0	2.22	12.9	3.51
	Thai Nguyen	3.8	0.98	10.4	1.84	18.3	2.31	18.8	2.09	29.7	3.66	19.1	4.00
	Phu Tho	2.4	0.59	11.3	1.81	19.5	2.35	22.4	2.17	28.3	2.66	16.2	3.61
	Vinh Phuc	5.3	1.06	18.1	2.34	22.7	2.01	20.1	1.84	22.5	2.56	11.3	3.06
	Bac Giang	4.5	1.08	16.2	2.03	26.1	2.05	22.2	1.67	22.2	2.39	8.8	2.18
	Bac Ninh	0.5	0.24	4.0	1.09	12.7	2.01	16.4	2.14	31.5	3.12	34.9	4.76
	Quang Ninh	0.3	0.20	4.0	1.05	11.0	2.16	14.9	2.06	32.8	3.88	37.0	5.71
North-West	Lai Chau	2.2	0.94	12.1	2.36	18.9	2.98	25.5	3.05	33.2	3.79	8.0	2.05
	Son La	8.7	2.29	16.3	2.49	22.6	2.87	19.2	3.19	23.9	3.77	9.5	2.79
	Hoa Binh	12.3	2.35	19.9	2.63	26.1	3.23	14.7	1.91	18.0	3.80	9.0	2.37
North-Central	Thanh Hoa	4.2	0.72	14.6	2.25	23.2	2.32	18.7	1.74	28.7	3.20	10.6	2.53
	Nghe An	6.7	1.72	12.1	1.75	22.7	2.62	18.8	1.89	26.7	3.35	13.1	3.50
	Ha Tinh	1.2	0.44	8.3	1.60	20.2	2.18	23.6	2.05	27.5	2.28	19.2	3.68
	Quang Binh	0.8	0.43	8.3	2.13	16.5	2.14	24.2	2.31	36.0	3.27	14.2	3.23
	Quang Tri	3.5	1.12	12.2	1.87	25.4	2.62	23.0	1.92	27.3	2.59	8.7	2.00
	Thua Thien-Huu	2.1	0.92	8.7	1.60	20.0	2.18	23.8	2.10	30.2	2.46	15.2	3.45

Central Coast	Da Nang	0.8	0.34	5.7	0.88	15.4	1.79	21.3	1.89	32.9	1.98	24.1	3.23
	Quang Nam	4.3	0.91	16.6	2.34	23.1	2.18	20.9	2.03	26.1	2.76	8.9	1.91
	Quang Ngai	7.1	1.61	20.2	2.44	27.5	2.36	17.4	1.68	18.4	2.11	9.5	2.52
	Binh Dinh	4.1	2.13	14.6	2.07	26.9	2.55	21.1	2.23	19.8	2.81	13.6	4.20
	Phu Yen	3.8	0.74	15.0	1.73	26.8	2.10	22.5	1.70	23.5	2.34	8.3	1.69
	Khanh Hoa	4.0	0.81	16.6	1.86	28.7	1.92	23.9	1.54	20.3	1.82	6.5	1.27
Central Highlands	Kon Tum	18.7	4.71	19.1	2.32	21.5	2.70	14.0	1.90	17.7	3.43	8.9	2.91
	Gia Lai	7.8	2.14	13.5	2.31	18.7	2.63	18.9	2.75	27.1	3.53	13.9	3.41
	Dak Lak	3.9	0.92	11.0	2.02	20.4	2.27	22.9	2.46	28.3	3.03	13.6	3.51
South-East	Ho Chi Minh	0.5	0.24	6.2	1.39	19.5	2.11	20.7	2.04	31.0	1.90	22.2	2.89
	Lam Dong	3.7	1.18	11.8	1.75	23.4	2.29	21.7	1.99	24.8	2.75	14.7	3.19
	Ninh Thuan	8.8	1.56	25.5	2.30	26.1	1.82	17.4	1.63	16.9	2.27	5.3	0.95
	Binh Phuoc	4.7	1.01	19.9	1.75	31.0	1.74	23.3	1.90	15.6	1.58	5.6	1.82
	Tay Ninh	4.8	0.95	18.9	2.34	28.5	2.23	22.8	2.53	19.7	2.44	5.4	1.48
	Binh Duong	1.6	0.53	8.3	1.26	24.1	2.22	22.9	2.02	29.2	2.71	13.9	2.69
	Dong Nai	2.4	0.78	9.1	1.42	25.9	1.65	26.2	1.63	25.8	1.82	10.5	1.27
	Binh Thuan	4.0	1.17	18.4	1.71	31.6	2.19	23.0	1.66	16.9	1.95	6.2	1.64
	Ba Ria-Vung Tau	1.0	0.39	7.9	1.20	26.9	2.17	24.6	1.61	28.8	2.15	10.8	2.02
Mekong Delta	Long An	3.9	1.09	17.0	2.12	28.0	1.89	26.5	2.29	20.3	2.32	4.3	1.25
	Dong Thap	6.0	1.30	23.1	2.63	26.8	2.26	18.5	2.28	18.0	2.87	7.6	2.41
	An Giang	9.0	1.67	24.3	2.87	26.7	2.50	18.6	2.23	13.9	2.19	7.6	2.38
	Tien Giang	2.8	0.70	13.4	2.00	28.8	2.49	20.2	1.80	22.4	2.46	12.5	2.78
	Vinh Long	4.1	0.91	18.7	1.93	23.5	1.82	20.4	1.73	21.9	2.27	11.5	3.00
	Ben Tre	2.9	0.72	13.8	1.57	28.0	2.30	24.7	1.56	21.8	2.22	8.9	2.02
	Kien Giang	9.6	1.70	27.6	2.48	30.3	2.00	12.8	1.38	13.4	2.37	6.3	2.35
	Can Tho	8.1	1.46	26.5	2.67	28.3	2.40	15.0	1.69	14.7	2.77	7.3	2.68
	Tra Vinh	11.2	1.58	32.3	2.78	27.8	2.29	13.2	1.96	12.6	2.26	2.9	1.49
	Soc Trang	13.1	2.36	29.0	2.67	28.6	2.30	16.3	1.94	11.0	2.65	2.0	0.85
	Bac Lieu	11.9	1.63	28.2	2.65	26.0	2.35	11.4	1.58	10.8	2.49	11.8	5.02
	Ca Mau	8.1	1.27	24.4	2.43	26.7	2.31	17.3	2.19	16.3	2.96	7.3	2.81
	Vietnam	4.6	0.17	14.4	0.28	23.1	0.34	20.2	0.27	24.5	0.39	13.1	0.41

Appendix 3. Countries participating in IEA, PISA and SACMEQ

Country	IEA	PISA	SACMEQ	Country	IEA	PISA	SACMEQ
Albania		x		Lebanon	x		
Argentina	x	x		Macao		x	
Armenia	x			Macedonia	x	x	
Australia	x	x		Malawi			x
Austria	x	x		Malaysia	x		
Azerbaijan		x		Mauritius			x
Bahrain	x			Mexico	x	x	
Belgium	x	x		Moldova	x		
Belize	x			Montenegro		x	
Bolivia				Morocco	x		
Botswana	x		x	Mozambique			x
Brazil		x		Namibia			x
Bulgaria	x	x		Netherlands	x	x	
Canada	x	x		New Zealand	x	x	
Chile	x	x		Nicaragua	x		
China	x	x		Norway	x	x	
Chinese Taipei	x	x		Palestinian Authority	x		
Colombia	x	x		Peru		x	
Croatia		x		Philippines	x	x	
Cyprus	x			Poland	x	x	
Czech Rep.	x	x		Portugal	x	x	
Denmark	x	x		Qatar		x	
Egypt	x			Romania	x	x	
Estonia	x	x		Russian Federation	x	x	
Finland	x	x		Saudi Arabia	x		
France	x	x		Serbia	x	x	
Germany	x	x		Seychelles			x

Ghana	x		Singapore	x		
Greece	x	x	Slovak Republic	x	x	
Hong Kong-China	x	x	Slovenia	x	x	
Hungary	x	x	South Africa	x		x
Iceland	x	x	Spain	x	x	
Indonesia	x	x	Swaziland			x
Iran	x		Sweden	x	x	
Ireland	x	x	Switzerland	x	x	
Israel	x	x	Syria	x		
Italy	x	x	Tanzania			x
Japan	x	x	Thailand	x	x	
Jordan	x	x	Tunisia	x	x	
Kenya		x	Turkey	x	x	
Korea	x	x	Uganda			x
Kuwait	x		United Kingdom	x	x	
Kyrgyzstan		x	United States	x	x	
Latvia	x	x	Uruguay		x	
Lesotho		x	Yemen	x		
Liechtenstein		x	Zambia			x
Lithuania	x	x	Zanzibar			x
Luxembourg	x	x	Zimbabwe			x

Appendix 4. General policy research questions for SACMEQ II

Theme A: Pupils' characteristics and their learning environments

General Policy Concern 1: What were the personal characteristics (for example, age and gender) and home background characteristics (for example, parent education, regularity of meals, home language, etc.) of grade 6 pupils that might have implications for monitoring equity, and/ or that might impact upon teaching and learning?

General Policy Concern 2: What were the school context factors experienced by grade 6 pupils (such as location, absenteeism (regularity and reasons), grade repetition and homework (frequency, amount, correction and family involvement)) that might impact upon teaching/learning and the general functioning of schools?

General Policy Concern 3: Did grade 6 pupils have sufficient access to classroom materials (for example, textbooks, readers and stationery) in order to participate fully in their lessons?

General Policy Concern 4: Did grade 6 pupils have access to library books within their schools, and (if they did have access) was the use of these books being maximized by allowing pupils to take them home to read?

General Policy Concern 5: Has the practice of grade 6 pupils receiving extra lessons in school subjects outside school hours become widespread, and have these been paid lessons?

Theme B: Teachers' characteristics and their viewpoints on teaching, classroom resources, professional support and job satisfaction

General Policy Concern 6: What were the personal characteristics of grade 6 teachers (for example, age, gender and socio-economic level) and what was the condition of their housing?

General Policy Concern 7: What were the professional characteristics of grade 6 teachers (in terms of academic, professional and in-service training) and did they consider in-service training to be effective in improving their teaching?

General Policy Concern 8: How did grade 6 teachers allocate their time among responsibilities concerned with teaching, preparing lessons and marking?

General Policy Concern 9: What were grade 6 teachers' viewpoints on (a) pupil activities within the classroom (for example, reading aloud, pronouncing, etc.), (b) teaching goals (for example, making learning enjoyable, word attack skills, etc.), (c) teaching approaches/strategies (for example, questioning, whole class teaching, etc.), (d) assessment procedures, and (e) meeting and communicating with parents?

General Policy Concern 10: What was the availability of classroom furniture (for example, sitting/writing places, teacher table, teacher chair and bookshelves) and classroom equipment (for example, chalkboard, dictionary, maps, book corner and teacher guides) in grade 6 classrooms?

General Policy Concern 11: What professional support (in terms of education resource centres, inspections, advisory visits and school head inputs) was given to grade 6 teachers?

General Policy Concern 12: What factors had most impact upon teacher job satisfaction?

*Theme C: School heads' characteristics
and their viewpoints on educational infrastructure,
the organization and operation of schools,
and problems with pupils and staff*

General Policy Concern 13: What were the personal characteristics of school heads (for example, age and gender)?

General Policy Concern 14: What were the professional characteristics of school heads (in terms of academic, professional, experience and specialized training)?

General Policy Concern 15: What were the school heads' viewpoints on general school infrastructure (for example, electrical and other equipment, water and basic sanitation) and the condition of school buildings?

General Policy Concern 16: What were the school heads' viewpoints on (a) daily activities (for example, teaching, school-community relations and monitoring pupil progress), (b) organizational policies (for example school magazine, open days and formal debates), (c) inspections, (d) community input, (e) problems with pupils and staff (for example, pupil lateness, teacher absenteeism and lost days of school)?

*Theme D: Equity in the allocation of human
and material resources among regions
and among schools within regions*

General Policy Concern 17: Have human resources (for example, qualified and experienced teachers and school heads) been allocated in an equitable fashion among regions and among schools within regions?

General Policy Concern 18: Have material resources (for example, classroom teaching materials and school facilities) been allocated in an equitable fashion among regions and among schools within regions?

Theme E: The reading and mathematics achievement levels of pupils and their teachers

General Policy Concern 19: What were the levels (according to descriptive levels of competence) and variations (among schools and regions) in the achievement levels of grade 6 pupils and their teachers in reading and mathematics – for my country and for all other SACMEQ countries?

General Policy Concern 20: What were the reading and mathematics achievement levels of important subgroups of grade 6 pupils and their teachers (for example, pupils and teachers of different genders, socio-economic levels and locations)?

Appendix 5. Items in characteristics as learners' scales in PISA

Learning strategies

Elaboration strategies

When I study, I try to relate new material to things I have learned in other subjects.

When I study, I figure out how the information might be useful in the real world.

When I study, I try to understand the material better by relating it to things I already know.

When I study, I figure out how the material fits in with what I have learned.

Memorization strategies

When I study, I try to memorize everything that might be covered.

When I study, I memorize as much as possible.

When I study, I memorize all new material so that I can recite it.

When I study, I practice by saying the material to myself over and over.

Control strategies

When I study, I start by figuring out what exactly I need to learn.

When I study, I force myself to check to see if I remember what I have learned.

When I study, I try to figure out, as I read, which concepts I still haven't really understood.

When I study, I make sure that I remember the most important things.

When I study and I don't understand something, I look for additional information to clarify the point.

Motivation

Instrumental motivation

I study to increase my job opportunities.
I study to ensure that my future will be financially secure.
I study to get a good job.

Interest in reading

Because reading is fun, I wouldn't want to give it up.
I read in my spare time.
When I read, I sometimes get totally absorbed.

Interest in mathematics

When I do mathematics, I sometimes get totally absorbed.
Mathematics is important to me personally.
Because doing mathematics is fun, I wouldn't want to give it up.

Effort and persistence in learning

When studying. I work as hard as possible.
When studying, I keep working even if the material is difficult.
When studying, I try to do my best to acquire the knowledge and skills taught.
When studying, I put forth my best effort.

Self-related beliefs

Self-efficacy

I'm certain I can understand the most difficult material presented in readings.
I'm confident I can understand the most complex material presented by the teacher.
I'm confident I can do an excellent job on assignments and tests.
I'm certain I can master the skills being taught.

Self-concept of verbal competencies

I'm hopeless in test language classes (*Reversed*).
When I do mathematics, I sometimes get totally absorbed.
Mathematics is important to me personally.
Because doing mathematics is fun, I wouldn't want to give it up.

Self-concept of mathematical competencies

I get good marks in mathematics.
Mathematics is one of my best subjects.
I have always done well in mathematics.

Academic self-concept

I learn things quickly in most school subjects.
I do well in tests in most school subjects.
I'm good at most school subjects.

Self-report of social competencies

Preference for co-operative learning
I like to work with other students.
I learn the most when I work with other students.
I do my best work when I work with other students.
I like to help other people do well in a group.
It is helpful to put together everyone's ideas when working on a project.

Preference for competitive learning

I like to try to be better than other students.
Trying to be better than others makes me work well.
I would like to be the best at something.
I learn faster if I'm trying to do better than the others.

Appendix 6. Percentage of correct items on whole test and subsets of items for selected countries

	Singapore	Japan	Korea	Hong Kong	Belgium (Fl)	Czech Republic	Slovak Republic	Switzerland	Austria	Hungary	France	Slovenia
(Number of score points included)												
162**	144	153	148	150	140	150	152	133	147	162	140	151
Singapore 79 (0.9)	79	79	80	79	79	79	79	80	80	79	79	79
Japan 73 (0.4)	73	73	74	73	73	73	73	75	74	73	73	73
Korea 72 (0.5)	71	72	73	72	71	72	71	72	72	72	71	71
Hong Kong 70 (1.4)	70	70	71	70	70	70	70	71	71	70	70	70
Belgium (Fl) 66 (1.4)	65	65	67	65	65 .	65	65	68	66	66	66	65
Czech Republic 66 (1.1)	65	66	67	66	66	66	66	68	66	66	66	66
Slovak Republic 62 (0.8)	63	63	64	63	63	63	63	65	63	62	63	63
Switzerland 62 (0.6)	61	62	63	61	61	61	62	64	62	62	62	61
Austria 62 (0.8)	62	62	63	62	61	62	62	64	62	62	62	61
Hungary 62 (0.7)	61	61	63	61	61	61	61	63	62	62	61	61
France 61 (0.8)	61	61	62	61	60	61	61	63	61	61	61	61
Slovenia 61 (0.7)	61	61	62	61	61	61	61	63	62	61	61	61

Appendix 7. The correlations of the person locations in reading test estimated with only the essential items of the curriculum of the countries

	Bot_S2	KEN_S1	KEN_S2	LES_S2	MAL_S1	MAL_S2	MAU_S1	MAU_S2	MOZ_S2	NAM_S1	NAM_S2	SEY_S2	SOU_S2	SWA_S2	TAN_S2	UGA_S2	ZAM_S1	ZAM_S2	ZAN_S1	ZAN_S2	ZIM_S1	ALL
Bot_S2	1.00																					
KEN_S1	0.99	1.00																				
KEN_S2	1.00	0.99	1.00																			
LES_S2	1.00	0.99	1.00	1.00																		
MAL_S1	0.99	0.99	0.99	0.99	1.00																	
MAL_S2	0.99	1.00	1.00	1.00	0.99	1.00																
MAU_S1	0.99	0.99	0.99	0.99	0.99	0.99	1.00															
MAU_S2	0.99	1.00	1.00	1.00	0.99	1.00	0.99	1.00														
MOZ_S2	0.99	1.00	1.00	1.00	0.99	1.00	0.99	1.00	1.00													
NAM_S1	0.98	0.98	0.98	0.98	0.98	0.98	0.99	0.98	0.99	1.00												
NAM_S2	0.99	1.00	1.00	1.00	0.99	1.00	0.99	1.00	1.00	0.98	1.00											
SEY_S2	0.99	1.00	1.00	1.00	0.99	1.00	0.99	1.00	1.00	0.98	1.00	1.00										
SOU_S2	0.99	1.00	1.00	1.00	0.99	1.00	0.99	1.00	1.00	0.99	1.00	1.00	1.00									
Swa_S2	0.99	0.99	0.99	0.99	0.99	0.99	0.99	0.99	1.00	0.98	0.99	0.99	0.99	1.00								
TAN_S2	0.99	1.00	1.00	1.00	0.99	1.00	0.99	1.00	1.00	0.99	1.00	1.00	1.00	1.00	1.00							
UGA_S2	0.99	1.00	1.00	1.00	0.99	1.00	0.99	1.00	1.00	0.99	1.00	1.00	1.00	1.00	1.00	1.00						
ZAM_S1	0.99	0.99	0.99	0.99	0.99	0.99	0.99	0.99	1.00	0.99	0.99	0.99	0.99	0.99	1.00	1.00	1.00					
ZAM_S2	0.99	0.99	0.99	0.99	0.99	0.99	0.99	0.99	0.99	0.98	0.99	0.99	0.99	0.99	0.99	0.99	0.99	1.00				
ZAN_S1	0.99	0.99	0.99	1.00	1.00	0.99	0.99	0.99	0.99	0.98	0.99	0.99	0.99	0.99	0.99	0.99	0.99	0.99	1.00			
ZAN_S2	0.99	0.99	0.99	0.99	0.99	0.99	0.99	0.99	1.00	0.99	0.99	0.99	0.99	1.00	0.99	0.99	1.00	0.99	0.99	1.00		
ZIM_S1	0.98	0.98	0.98	0.98	0.98	0.98	0.98	0.98	0.99	0.97	0.98	0.98	0.98	0.98	0.99	0.99	0.98	0.98	0.98	0.98	1.00	
All	1.00	0.99	1.00	1.00	0.99	1.00	0.99	1.00	1.00	0.99	1.00	1.00	1.00	1.00	1.00	1.00	1.00	0.99	0.99	0.99	0.99	1.00

IIEP publications and documents

More than 1,200 titles on all aspects of educational planning have been published by the International Institute for Educational Planning. A comprehensive catalogue is available in the following subject categories:

Educational planning and global issues
General studies – global/developmental issues

Administration and management of education
Decentralization – participation – distance education – school mapping – teachers

Economics of education
Costs and financing – employment – international co-operation

Quality of education
Evaluation – innovation – supervision

Different levels of formal education
Primary to higher education

Alternative strategies for education
Lifelong education – non-formal education – disadvantaged groups – gender education

Copies of the Catalogue may be obtained on request from:
IIEP, Communication and Publications Unit
information@iiep.unesco.org
Titles of new publications and abstracts may be consulted
at the following web site: www.unesco.org/iiep The International
Institute for Educational Planning

The International Institute for Educational Planning

The International Institute for Educational Planning (IIEP) is an international centre for advanced training and research in the field of educational planning. It was established by UNESCO in 1963 and is financed by UNESCO and by voluntary contributions from Member States. In recent years the following Member States have provided voluntary contributions to the Institute: Denmark, Finland, Germany, Iceland, India, Ireland, Norway, Sweden and Switzerland.

The Institute's aim is to contribute to the development of education throughout the world, by expanding both knowledge and the supply of competent professionals in the field of educational planning. In this endeavour the Institute co-operates with interested training and research organizations in Member States. The Governing Board of the IIEP, which approves the Institute's programme and budget, consists of a maximum of eight elected members and four members designated by the United Nations Organization and certain of its specialized agencies and institutes.

Inquiries about the Institute should be addressed to:
The Office of the Director, International Institute for Educational Planning,
7-9 rue Eugène Delacroix, 75116 Paris, France.